D1030614

How
To Read The
Bible

How To Read The Bible

By
Edgar J. Goodspeed

The John C. Winston Company
PHILADELPHIA   TORONTO

To

WILLIAM LINCOLN HONNOLD
Wise Counselor

and

Generous Friend

ACKNOWLEDGMENTS

For Hebrew history and law I have made much use of the published work of my friend Dr. Robert H. Pfeiffer, of Harvard University. I gratefully make acknowledgment also to the authors and publishers who have permitted the quotation of passages from their copyrighted publications:

The Complete Bible: An American Translation, edited by J. M. Powis Smith and Edgar J. Goodspeed. Published, 1935. All quotations from this book are reprinted by permission of The University of Chicago Press.

"Word Makers" in *No Traveller Returns,* by Joseph Auslander. 1933. Published by Harper & Brothers.

PREFACE

The Bible is rich in literary, historical, and religious treasures, which many of us fail to find for want of a little direction in the search for them. We find ourselves dismayed at the sheer bulk of the Bible, for one thing—eleven hundred pages of double-column fine print. Its books are, moreover, of a perplexing range and variety, and the most familiar and interesting do not stand at the beginning.

It is this state of things that deters so many modern readers from attempting the Bible. They respect it and want to know it, but they are disinclined to plow through seven hundred and fifty pages before they get to the part that really interests them most. There must be a better way to get acquainted with the great library which we call the Bible and to find out its principal riches and values.

Let us then undertake a literary and historical approach to it, taking up the chief books in it as biography, oratory, history, poetry, drama, fiction, letters, and visions, in the light of the times that produced them and the purposes of their writers, thus combining literary and historical interests, always remembering that important as they undoubtedly are for literature and history, their religious messages must be kept uppermost, since it was chiefly to promote that side of life that they were written.

Many readers who have looked upon the Bible as a huge book too antique and portentous to interest them may, we hope, come to see it as a rich and varied library, to find their way about among its masterpieces and feel at home among them, and to make friends with the prophets who so largely wrote it, and, above all, with its last great Hero, who called his followers his friends.

This book is intended not as a summary of the Bible or as a substitute for it but as a companion and guide to the reading of it. It does not attempt to epitomize its contents but to help the reader to find its chief treasures for himself.

Edgar J Goodspeed

TABLE OF CONTENTS

Whatever other uses men may wish to make of the Bible, our first and paramount duty is to READ IT.

— Richard Green Moulton.

CHAPTER ONE

Where to Begin

THE OBVIOUS way to read a book is to begin at the beginning and read it through; to look at the end to see how it is coming out is weakness.

But the Bible is not a book; it is a library. How do you read a library? Certainly not by taking the catalog and reading first the first book listed in it, then the second, and so on. Nor do you read it shelf by shelf, beginning at the upper left-hand corner. You follow some definite interest of yours, or you decide upon some principle to guide your reading.

The Bible has all the range and variety of a library. It was written on two continents, in three languages, by a hundred authors, scattered over a thousand years. Not only Egypt and Babylon, Palestine and Syria, but Greece and Rome witnessed its origins. Its various parts reflect widely different levels of morals and civilization.

Its very name declares it is a library, for it is just a modern form of the Greek word *Biblia*, which meant "papyrus scrolls," the prevalent book-form of antiquity. In the early days of Christianity, men had not learned how to assemble all of the Old Testament, or even all of Homer into one book. As they knew the Bible, it took forty or fifty scrolls to accommodate

1

its eighty books. It was in fact as well as in name a library—
The Books, par excellence.

As these sixty-six or, with the Apocrypha, eighty books are
bound today, the New Testament stands at the end of the
Bible, but it is the end from which most of us approach it.
We begin with the New Testament. We hear about the
Golden Rule, the Lord's Prayer, the Beatitudes, and the
Sermon on the Mount long before we become interested in
Adam and Eve, Noah and Abraham, or Joseph and his
brethren. Nor do the kings and prophets of Israel ever equal
in their interest and value to us the figures of Jesus and his
chief apostles.

The teachings of the Old Testament, too, lofty as many of
them are, do not come home to our consciences as those of
Jesus do, and the problems that concerned the prophets never
fit into our religious experiences as do those dealt with in the
Four Gospels or the letters of Paul. The world of Jesus is
much closer to our own than that of the ancient Hebrews can
possibly be, no matter how hard we try to understand it and
sympathize with it.

And the Gospels speak a much plainer language, both of
fact and of symbol, than do the prophets or even the Psalms.
The Twenty-third Psalm is indeed dear to the hearts of mankind, but hardly dearer than the fourteenth chapter of John.
Generally speaking, few of the parables call for much explanation for us, while few of the sayings of the prophets do
not.

Above all, the New Testament as a whole meets us on a
far higher moral and religious level than the Old. It calls us
upward to the plane on which we ought to live, and want to
live. It offers us a great religious experience of faith, hope, and

love, and it makes it irresistibly attractive, as the Old Testament, with all its arts of rhetoric, never did.

So it is right to approach the Bible by way of the New Testament. But how shall we approach the New Testament? Shall we begin with Matthew because it stands first, at the portal?

No, let us begin with the Gospel of Mark. Not because it is older by a few years than Matthew's, nor because Matthew repeats almost all of it in his, but because it is the most narrative of the Gospels; it most vividly tells a story. And what a story! The great tragedy; heroic tragedy at its best and greatest, all the more so because it is not just the elaborate fancy of some gifted artist, Shakespeare or Dante, but the unvarnished truth told as Mark had been told it by those who had seen the action it records. Told in the ancient religious vocabulary of demon and marvel, it is still in its main outlines convincing and moving beyond any other narrative ever written. Told by a man who was not shaping his information to some pattern of his own, or guided by any rules of literary art, but humbly seeking to suggest something too great for him to fathom, and beyond his powers to create or to control, and writing to preserve from his memories of the reports of eyewitnesses already dead, it is a story too great to be allowed to perish. Indeed, Mark is less a gospel than the materials out of which more studied and finished gospels were later written, by men who realized the use that could be made of it for ends they clearly saw.

THE GOSPEL OF MARK

Let us begin the reading of the Bible with the Gospel of Mark, and let us read it not piecemeal, as if it were very difficult; the Gospels are as a matter of fact very easy reading, full of interest and action. Among the Greek manuscripts of the New Testament, those of the Gospels are much more numerous than those of any other part or of the whole, and even today the Gospels are sold and read in much greater numbers than any other parts of the Bible. If we ask, "How is the Gospel of Mark to be read?" the answer is, "At one sitting," as any close-packed, swiftly moving story should be read. It can easily be read aloud in an hour and a half, and to oneself in half that time.

Mark consists in the main of a number of apparently detached incidents, in each of which Jesus does or says something of great significance. The attentive reader will observe that the shadow of the cross falls across the pages almost from the beginning, and that Jesus soon perceives his danger and three times retreats before it. But at length he turns upon his foes and critics, prepares to face them at their great festival and in their stronghold, and sets out for Jerusalem, to make one great decisive effort to win his people to his gospel, and take the consequences. Let us read this incomparable story through, for once at least, at a single sitting, and hear what it has to say.

THE GOSPEL OF MATTHEW

The Gospel of Mark had been in circulation only ten or a dozen years when it was expanded into a larger book, the Gospel of Matthew. It repeated almost every line of Mark, but so filled in the picture with Jesus' sayings and teachings that he now appeared not so much as a Doer or Man of Action, but as a Teacher. In fact, the main literary feature of Matthew is a series of six sermons in which it casts the teaching of Jesus.

The first of these is the Sermon on the Mount, the most striking and comprehensive statement of Christian ethics ever
made. Here are found the Beatitudes, the Golden Rule, the
Lord's Prayer. Matthew saw in Jesus' teaching the program
for a new order in human society, a new relationship among
men, which he called the Kingdom of Heaven. The sermon
fills chs. 5; 6; and 7.

The teaching is resumed in ch. 10, with instructions about
how to preach the gospel. The third sermon, ch. 13, is a collection of parables, that is, figures or stories, on the growth
of the Kingdom. Chapter 18 tells of humility and forgiveness,
and ch. 23 denounces the hypocrisies of Pharisaic religion, but
ends with the touching lament over Jerusalem:

"O Jerusalem, Jerusalem! murdering the prophets, and
stoning those who are sent to her, how often I have longed to
gather your children around me, as a hen gathers her brood
under her wings, but you refused! Now I leave you to your-
selves. For I tell you, you will never see me again until you
say, 'Blessed be he who comes in the Lord's name!' "

The final discourse, chs. 24 and 25, foretells the destruction of Jerusalem and the end of the world. Chapter 25 consists of three parables—the Bridesmaids, the Talents, and the
Last Judgment. In this final parable the moral teaching of
Matthew reaches its climax with the words, "In so far as you
failed to do it for one of these people who are humblest, you
failed to do it for me."

The curtain falls on the Gospel of Matthew with Jesus
reunited with his disciples as a spiritual presence, to remain
with them to the very end. He had preached to the Jews
alone, but they are to carry his message to foreign lands.
Certainly the Gospel of Matthew is a much more consciously

and purposefully organized book than that of Mark. Renan, the French historian, said it was the most important book in the world.

Read the Gospel of Matthew for its striking picture of the teaching of Jesus, set against the background of contemporary Pharisaic teaching, in the six great discourses, chs. 5 to 7; 10; 13; 18; 23; and 24–25.

THE GOSPEL OF LUKE

Luke, like Matthew, includes a genealogy of Jesus, and tells of his infancy and something of his youth. From his story of the angels and the shepherds he has been called the "Man Who Gave Us Christmas." What we call his Gospel was really the first volume of his two-volume work on the beginnings of Christianity, The Acts being the second volume, and presents Jesus as the Founder of a new religion, Christianity. Luke's historical interest led him to give us one definite date, in the usual Greek fashion, by the regnal year of the Roman emperor. It was the date of the call of John the Baptist to preach, in the fifteenth year of Tiberius or A.D. 29 (Luke 3:1). To him we also owe our introduction to Christian psalmody, for he it was who preserved for us the canticles on the Nativity, chs. 1 and 2. Besides these historical and literary interests, Luke evinces also a keen humanitarian concern, for it is he who records the Parable of the Good Samaritan, called by modern philanthropists the most characteristically Christian of the parables. The Prodigal Son and the Rich Man and Lazarus are other parables that we owe to Luke. Like Matthew, Luke made copious use of the Gospel of Mark; in fact, he followed Mark's order very closely, but his Gospel is very different from Matthew's, with less concern about the religion of the Pharisees and more interest in the social, humanitarian, and universal aspects of Jesus' teaching. When he wrote, Christianity had already passed out of Jewish hands and was making great progress among the Greeks who were widely scattered through the Roman Empire. Luke was less a biographer than a historian, for his purpose was the larger one of showing how from the life and work of Jesus had sprung a new religion that promised to win the world. We shall think of him again in this broader aspect when we consider the later histories in the Bible. For Luke was the first historian of Christianity and the founder of church history. But the first volume of his history was so complete in itself that when the Four Gospels were collected and published about A.D. 115–120, it was brought into the collection as one of them.

THE GOSPEL OF JOHN

The latest of the Four Gospels in date is the Gospel of John. It reflects two generations of Christian reflection and experience. Jesus had proved to be far more than the Messiah of Jewish expectation; through the storm and stress of persecution, Christians had found in him a great spiritual reinforcement, indeed a new religious life altogether. Christianity was a new birth, and the Christian found himself transported to a new world. Instead of the brutal pagan scene about him, full of darkness, hatred, death, ignorance, and bondage, he lived in a realm of light, love, life, truth, knowledge, and freedom. It was indeed a new climate that he now enjoyed, one that he had not supposed existed in the world. And he

had reached it through Jesus. It was Jesus who had revealed
it, and embodied it, and given his life to communicate it to
mankind. So Jesus was a Savior. He was the Bread of Life
and the Light of the World. It is this splendid consciousness
of what Jesus had come to mean to human life that John
reads back into his earthly ministry, and in the light of the
Christian centuries, we cannot call it an exaggeration. John
said that Jesus' Spirit would lead his followers on to greater
deeds than he had done and would guide them into fuller and
fuller knowledge of the truth, startling statements which time
has strangely fulfilled. The Spirit of Truth would guide them
into the full truth. "You will know the truth and the truth
will set you free." (John 8:32.) With all this great concern for light, knowledge, truth, and freedom, John is
deeply concerned for the Christian's personal inner life, and
his communion with the overshadowing, all-pervasive spirit
of God, that "conversation with the universe," which is so
much the largest part of every conscious existence. That is to
be his great source of strength and comfort, his constant reinforcement. God loves the world, and forgives it; he does not
hate it. Jesus hails his followers as his friends, not his slaves,
and welcomes them to a new order of friendship and love.

Read the Gospel of John for its picture of what the Christian gospel meant to Greek believers all over the Roman
world; for its recognition of Jesus as the embodiment of the
highest Wisdom of God and at the same time the guide and
helper of the individual human spirit.

We must begin the Bible with the Gospels, for the rest
of it must be read from no lower point of view. Possessed
with the moral and religious ideas of the Gospels, humility,
forgiveness, aspiration, purity of heart, faith, and good will

to all mankind, one can read the darkest pages of the Old Testament or the Apocrypha with tolerance and understanding. We can look down with compassion upon the harshness and cruelty that men of old times permitted themselves in the name of God, for we have seen a nobler and better way. We can recognize the struggle toward truth and justice and goodness they were so slowly making. At the same time we will find in their long, bitter, and bloody conflict many a word and deed that will speak powerfully to our own religious experience and moral needs.

CHAPTER TWO

Biographies

ALTHOUGH THE most striking and influential books in the Bible, the Four Gospels, are in the field of biography, the ancient Hebrews seldom if ever wrote biographies. They had their great heroes and had much that was biographical to say about them, but they cared much more about the periods in men's lives when they were actively engaged in shaping great events than they were in telling all about their youth, education, how they felt, and everything that happened to them. They were interested in great personalities and their impact upon their times, and their stories have never been more vividly and forcefully told. But they were told simply as part of the record of broader historical movements, into which they were woven.

JOSEPH

One of the greatest of these is the story of Joseph, the elder of Jacob's sons by Rachel. It had long been preserved by word of mouth among Joseph's descendants in the tribes or half-tribes of Ephraim and Manasseh, which dominated the northern part of Israel especially after the division of the kingdom, about 933 B.C., but it was written down as part of a longer record about the middle of the eighth century before Christ, 750 B.C. We find it embodied in the later chapters of Genesis, 37 and 39 to 50. It is a romantic story of poetic justice and brilliant success in life in the face of the greatest obstacles; of supreme wisdom as food administrator in the most fertile country in the world.

MOSES

The most commanding figure in the Old Testament is Moses, the emancipator and lawgiver of the Hebrews and the first of the prophets, that amazing series of speakers for God which more than anything else distinguished the Jewish people. The prophets were not predictors of future events but spokesmen for morality and reformation, voices within the nation fearlessly condemning the evils of their times in the name of God. The first of these, and the founder of the order, was Moses. So great was his influence upon Jewish life that all their laws of whatever date were instinctively ascribed to him.

If any Old Testament character deserved a biography, certainly Moses did, but his story is so interwoven with Jewish laws of different periods that it can hardly be extricated. How he escaped death in infancy, was adopted by a princess and taught all that the Egyptians knew, and then heroically stood up against the might of Pharaoh and got his people safely out of Egypt is one of the greatest stories in the world. But it simply leads up to the climax, the giving of the law at Sinai, Exodus, chs. 1 to 20. All the rest of the Pentateuch, with all its various laws for priesthood and people, is worked into the life of Moses, but the more biographical parts are in Exodus,

chs. 24 and 31 to 35; in Numbers, 10:11 to 14:45; chs. 16;
17; 20; 21; 25; and 27, and Deuteronomy, ch. 34.

JOSHUA

Moses' attendant and successor Joshua is mentioned here
and there in the Pentateuch, as the general of the Hebrews
in the battle with the Amalekites, when Aaron and Hur held
Moses' hands up, to insure victory; as the prophet's attendant when Moses approached Mount Sinai, the mountain of
God, Ex. 24:13; 32:17; and as one of the spies sent ahead to
spy out the Promised Land, Num. 13:8. He does not take
the center of the stage, however, until the opening of the book
that bears his name. In it he is throughout the chief figure,
as he goes about the invasion and conquest of the Promised
Land of Canaan, from the day the walls of Jericho fell down,
ch. 6:20, to his final muster of the tribes at Shechem for his
solemn farewell, ch. 24. The Book of Joshua must stand as
one of the most biographical of the Old Testament books. All
that separates it from true biography is the fact that its chief
concern is not with Joshua and his fortunes but with the
Hebrew people and their religion, and with Joshua only in
proportion to his importance to them.

DAVID

A much clearer piece of biography in the Old Testament
is found in the latter half of I Samuel and the whole of
II Samuel, which tell the inimitable story of David, the idol
of the Hebrew people and their great hero. Indeed, if we were
to name the books of Samuel, we would call them the books

of David, for they are much more concerned with him than
with Samuel, whose death is reported in I Sam. 25:1. David
is first mentioned in ch. 16, but from that point on he rapidly
becomes the leading figure of the story, chs. 16 to 31, and
continues to hold the stage all through II Samuel. In fact,
his death is not related until the first and second chapters of
I Kings, where his wife Bathsheba prevails upon the dying
king to name her son Solomon as his successor.

The biographical sketch of David in I and II Samuel and
I Kings takes up more of the Old Testament than is given to
any other character in it, about fifty pages, or one-seventeenth
of the whole. And since it deals with his youth, maturity, and
old age, and views his character dispassionately, the good and
bad sides alike, it may be considered the nearest approach to
biography that the Hebrews achieved. If we add the space
devoted to him in I Chronicles, seventeen pages, the total is
sixty-seven pages, or about one-thirteenth of the Old Testament, to say nothing of the psalms ascribed to him in the
Psalter.

We cannot help wondering who among David's contemporaries could have composed and even written this narrative,
or the basis of it. It is remarkable in that it does not idealize
David, but frankly records his base and selfish behavior about
Bathsheba, while telling the wonderful series of hero stories
that have made David such a popular figure. It is so graphic
and well informed that one can almost think it the work of
David's priest Abiathar, whose father Ahimelech was put to
death for sheltering David when he was a fugitive. Abiathar
had escaped his father's fate and taken refuge with David in
the cave of Adullam, sharing his perils from that time on, and
no one can deny that David lived dangerously. When David

died, and Solomon did away with his whole staff, Abiathar was spared, being exiled to the town of Anathoth, not far from Jerusalem. It is not difficult to imagine his spending his old age recording his memories, good and bad, of his great captain. But this, of course, is only conjecture. The Hebrews did not often name their authors, and the books of Samuel and Kings are anonymous.

So, for the life of David, read I Samuel, chs. 16 to 31, all of II Samuel, and the first and second chapters of I Kings. I Chronicles has a shorter parallel account, chs. 11 to 29, but they add little to what these forty-two chapters have to tell of the life of David.

SOLOMON

The career of David's son and successor, Solomon, so famous for his wisdom, is the subject of the first eleven chapters of I Kings. It is also recorded in the first nine chapters of II Chronicles, but with much less fulness; in fact, the Chronicles account is only half the length of that in Kings. Read the story of Solomon, therefore, in I Kings, chs. 1 to 11. In literary and in historical value it is altogether the better of the two. As compared with the story of David in the books of Samuel, it lacks the adventurous epic quality that so strongly marks the story of David. Solomon is not at all the chivalrous hero, but the typical oriental monarch, of the better kind.

ELIJAH, ELISHA

More than half a century after Solomon's time, the figure of Elijah appears, towering above all his Hebrew contemporaries. He was a prophet of the Northern Kingdom of Israel, and was most active between 875 and 850 B.C. He declared that no god but Jehovah should be worshiped within the borders of Israel, and he maintained this with the most fiery courage. Little of his teaching was recorded; it was his deeds that enforced his doctrine, and the stories of what he did are scattered through the books of Kings from I Kings, chapter 17, to II Kings, chapter 2. His work in the Northern Kingdom of Israel was carried on in the latter half of the ninth century by his disciple Elisha, whose wonders fill most of II Kings, chapters 2 to 9 and 13. The stories of these great ninth-century prophets were written down probably between 800 and 750 B.C., those of Elijah with especial literary skill, and were later wrought into the books of Kings. They are, of course, not actual biographies, but they are biographical fragments and reflect a further biographical interest among the Hebrews.

ISAIAH

The literary prophets whose utterances have been preserved under their respective names, from Amos and Hosea on, tell us something of their lives and fortunes, but far less than what we might expect. Their books are not biographies but oracles, with very little personal information, and yet they are full of the prophet's inner experiences, and so in the deeper sense highly autobiographical. Each book naturally reveals something of its writer, and sometimes there are a few chapters about the writer's life, as in Isaiah, chs. 6 to 8; 20; 36 to 39. The rest of Isaiah chs. 1 to 39 consists almost entirely of his poetical oracles.

JEREMIAH

The personal parts of Jeremiah are chs. 1; 7; 11; 12 to
21; 24 to 29; 32 to 44; and 51:59–64. Yet the whole
religious experience of Jeremiah was intensely personal, as he
saw his nation perish, and learned the hard lesson that religion
was a personal, not a national, matter, and that his faith could
survive his nation's downfall.

The Book of Jeremiah begins with the striking account of
his call to be a prophet, ch. 1, and his dismay at the approach
of the Scythians in 627 B.C. The finding of Deuteronomy, and
Josiah's reformation, in 621 B.C., fell in Jeremiah's early
years, but he seems to have taken little part in that movement, and even to have opposed it. Evidently he felt that it
made too much of ritual instead of the purity of heart that
he considered all-important.

Beyond most of the prophets, Jeremiah faced personal
peril. Early in Jehoiakim's reign, soon after 607 B.C., Jeremiah's Temple address, forecasting the destruction of Jerusalem, nearly cost him his life, ch. 26, and late in the same
reign, in 605 B.C., a Temple priest put him in the stocks for
the night, 20:1–3. In December, 604 B.C., King Jehoiakim,
on hearing the scroll of Jeremiah's early prophecies read,
burned it with his own hands, ch. 36. Jeremiah now went into
hiding, and for the remaining seven years of Jehoiakim's
reign, 604 to 597 B.C., must have been in constant danger of
death. The Babylonian conquerors, after taking the city in
597 B.C., made Zedekiah king, and early in his reign Jeremiah was consigned to a dungeon. When released from it, he

was still kept a prisoner in the court of the guard, ch. 37. What some considered his defeatist attitude led his opponents to lower him into an abandoned cistern to die, but a friend intervened and had him hauled out again and returned to the court of the guard, 38:6–13. There he remained until the second capture of the city by the Babylonians, 586 B.C., when he was assigned to a group of exiles bound for Babylon. But upon Nebuchadnezzar's order he was released and told to go where he pleased, chs. 39:11, 12; 40:4. The Babylonians now destroyed Jerusalem and the Temple, but Jeremiah chose to remain with the new governor, Gedaliah. Unfortunately, Gedaliah was soon assassinated, and Jeremiah and Baruch were carried off by the frightened remnant of the people to Daphne in Egypt, where he seems to have ended his stormy days, 43:4–7.

EZEKIEL

The later life of Ezekiel, the priest who in exile became a prophet, is sketched in Ezek. 1:1–3; ch. 3; 24:15–27; and 33:21–33.

NEHEMIAH

Another book like Joshua, bearing the name of its hero, is Nehemiah. Nehemiah was the cupbearer of King Artaxerxes, at Susa, in the twentieth year of his reign, 444 B.C. From him Nehemiah obtained a leave of absence to enable him to rebuild the walls of Jerusalem. This he accomplished in fifty-two days, but he continued as governor for twelve years, dividing his time between Jerusalem and the Persian capital. At any rate, he returned to Jerusalem as governor in 432, after some years' absence.

The Book of Nehemiah is his account, written in the first person singular, of his experiences and accomplishments in this period of his life. It is in form, at least, an autobiography, or a fragment of one. The animated personal story is interrupted by a very different section, full of genealogies, the reading of the law by Ezra, and a census of Jerusalem, Neh. 7:6 to 12:26, but at 12:27 the narrative of Nehemiah's work is resumed and he reappears in the first person in 12:31 and continues to speak for himself throughout the rest of the book. For the autobiography of Nehemiah, therefore, read Neh. 1:1 to 7:5 and 12:27 to 13:31.

This is generally accepted by scholars as a genuine piece of autobiography. But it begins very abruptly, in the twentieth year of Artaxerxes, and breaks off just as sharply with Nehemiah's ejection from the city of the grandson of the high priest, for marrying a foreign woman. Official autobiographies were frequent in Egypt and in Mesopotamia. The famous inscription of Darius I on the rock of Behistun is a nearer parallel; it has recently turned up in an Aramaic translation. But whether the book is by Nehemiah himself or by some Hebrew admirer, it is a vivid contemporary account of Nehemiah's work in Jerusalem, and from a literary if not a historical point of view is an autobiography. The grief of Nehemiah over the news of the dilapidated condition of Jerusalem, his ride about the ruined walls by night, and his humane social measures make a strong appeal to the modern reader, while his record-breaking feat of rebuilding the city walls in seven and a half weeks is of peculiar interest to our hustling age.

JESUS

It is as we enter the New Testament that the great examples of biography confront us in the Four Gospels, most commandingly in the quartet taken together. We must briefly review them here, in their place near the end of the Biblical biographies. They present different approaches to the life and significance of Jesus in religion and supplement each other in many ways. When we approach them as a biography, we may consider them as the ancients did as the Gospel—the part by Matthew, the part by Mark, the part by Luke, and the part by John. In the Early Church, they together formed the Gospel, for by A.D. 120 they were being published as a collection, making the composite picture of Jesus that we know so well.

Taken separately, it is clear at once that Mark is no adequate biography of Jesus. It introduces him as a grown man, and its whole narrative seems to cover only the short period of his public ministry, one or perhaps two years. It says nothing about his birth or youth. Yet for the time it covers, Mark seems nearer to the events it records than either of the others. Historically it therefore stands first.

Matthew is much more a biography. It presents a genealogy, tracing Jesus' ancestry back through Joseph and the kings of Judah to Abraham. It preserves stories of His birth and infancy, and then passes to his baptism and his call to his work. That work as Matthew viewed it was to set up on earth a new social and moral order, the Kingdom of Heaven. Its standards are presented in the Sermon on the Mount. The other five sermons into which Matthew gathered the teachings of Jesus present various aspects of this great conception. This series of sermons Matthew interweaves with the events of Jesus' ministry, very much as Mark had reported them.

Luke, too, offers a genealogy of Jesus, and tells of his infancy and youth. But he can hardly have meant his Gospel as a biography, for he makes it simply the first of his two volumes on the beginnings of Christianity, as he indicates in his preface, 1:1–4, and in Acts 1:1 and 2. So Luke presents Jesus as also the Founder of Christianity. His first volume has been made to serve as a biography by being separated from its companion volume, The Acts, and grouped with the other Gospels.

John approaches the work of Jesus from a Greek point of view, and his book is really as much a dialog as a Gospel, for he describes Jesus as engaging in long conversations with his hearers and opponents. What he had come to mean in Christian experience is now read back into his life. John finds in Jesus far more than the Messiah of Jewish expectation; he declares him to be the Light and Savior of the World. He presents the gospel in terms of light, love, life, truth, knowledge, freedom, which are still the great rallying cries of mankind.

The Four Gospels taken together not only present the loftiest moral ideals and demands ever set forth, but they also depict the most challenging and commanding religious leader who has appeared in history. Read Mark, for a historical close-up picture of Jesus as a Doer, a Man of Action. Then read Matthew for its account of Jesus as a Teacher and

of what he taught. Then read Luke for Jesus as the Founder
of a far-reaching religious movement, which we know as
Christianity. Then read John for what Jesus means in religious
experience, as Friend, Helper, Inspirer, Enlightener, and
Savior.

PETER

Foremost among Jesus' twelve apostles was Peter, who
at once after the crucifixion became the leader of Jesus' followers. He bitterly repented his denial of Jesus and atoned
for it by his subsequent courageous devotion. Although he is
mentioned more than a hundred times in the Gospels, through
the first twelve chapters of The Acts he is the leading figure
and he reappears in that rôle in ch. 15. His memories of Jesus
became the basis of the earliest Gospel. His service in rallying
Jesus' disciples and carrying on his work was of the utmost
importance, but in the narrative of The Acts he presently dis-
appears behind the figure of Paul, the leader of the mission
to the Greek world, which Luke regarded as of supreme importance. About Peter, then, we have only a biographical
fragment on a great dynamic personality, for whose later story
we are dependent upon sources outside the New Testament.

PAUL

Another figure for whom the New Testament offers substantial biographical material, though no individual biography, is the Apostle Paul. In the second volume of Luke's
history, known to us as The Acts of the Apostles, he is introduced (7:58) as the official representative of the Sanhedrin

at the stoning of Stephen. He is mentioned again in a similar capacity in 8:1, but with the beginning of the ninth chapter he comes definitely to the front, 9:1–30; he is brought actively into the Christian movement in 11:19–30, and from the beginning of chapter 13 to the end of The Acts he holds the center of the stage. The story of his experiences as he moves out into the Greek world as a missionary and visits one after another of the thriving cities of the Roman Empire from Jerusalem to Rome, constitutes one of the most detailed and illuminating biographical sketches that have come down to us from antiquity. His trials, his speeches, his travels, his voyages, never related for themselves but always for their bearing on the progress of the movement he championed, throw light on many phases of life in the Greco-Roman world of the empire, and in themselves possess an extraordinary degree of human interest. The reader finds himself taking Paul's part, and definitely on his side. The speeches are sometimes partly autobiographical, such as the one before the mob in Jerusalem, and the later one before Agrippa at Cæsarea, chs. 22; 26. These speeches we must consider elsewhere as examples of ancient oratory.

Paul has been called Luke's hero, and while that is an overstatement, Paul does assume heroic proportions in the narrative of the second half of The Acts, and his story shows Luke at his best as a biographer. He has really made us feel better acquainted with the Apostle Paul than with any other character in the Bible except Jesus. His letters (which are never mentioned in The Acts) contribute immensely to our knowledge of him, but it is Luke's narrative that has really told his story. It is really Biblical biography at its best.

For the biography of Paul read Acts 7:58; 8:1; 9:1–30;

11:19–30; and 13:1 to 28:31. With Luke as your guide follow him about the great splendid cities of the Greco-Roman world, Jerusalem, Damascus, Antioch, Tarsus, Athens, Corinth, Ephesus, Rome, and trace his missionary journeys, the First, from Antioch to Cyprus and southern Galatia, Acts, chs. 13 and 14.

On his Second Journey, Acts 15:36 to 18:22, setting out from Antioch, he traveled to Galatia, Troas, and Macedonia, where he visited Philippi, Thessalonica, and Berea; then to Greece, preaching at Athens, and finally reaching Corinth, where he wrote his two letters to the Thessalonians, A.D. 50–51. He returned from Corinth to Cæsarea by sea, touching at Ephesus on the way. Soon after, he wrote the letter to the Galatians.

On his Third Journey, Acts 18:23 to 21:3, Paul set out from Antioch and traveled through Asia Minor to Ephesus, where he spent more than two years, writing probably three letters to the Corinthians from that city. He went on to Macedonia, where he wrote his final letter to Corinth, probably our II Cor., chs. 1 to 9. Then he proceeded to Corinth, where he wrote the letter to the Romans, then took ship and sailed back by way of Philippi, Troas, and Miletus to Tyre.

Even more impressive was his final journey, Acts 27:1 to 28:16, the voyage to Rome, for trial before the emperor's court. His party sailed from Cæsarea, by way of Myra, Crete, and Malta, where they were wrecked and passed the winter, proceeding to Neapolis (Naples) in the spring, and thence up the Campanian and Appian Ways to Rome. At Rome, Paul wrote his letters to Philippi, Colossæ, and Philemon.

CHAPTER THREE

Speeches, Orations, and Sermons

THE HEBREWS were great orators. Their very poets were orators, for most of their poets were prophets, and when they rose to real heights of eloquence their sermons were poems. Even their drama, if we can call it that, was a series of great orations; some of those in Job perhaps the greatest ever uttered. Job is principally a series of fifteen speeches, all poetry. But the Hebrews used prose, too, in their appeals, speeches, and exhortations, and the bulk of Deuteronomy is a great speech, an hour and a quarter long. The Hebrews were so fond of oratory that they cast their entire law in the form of speeches, uttered by God to Moses, or by Moses to the people, the priests, or the elders. Being an ancient people, their whole literary expression was dominated and colored by the spoken word. And their vivid imaginations, dramatic sense, and depth of feeling gave their eloquence an emotional quality that has never been surpassed. For, as John Bright once said, "Eloquence is emotion."

One of the most moving speeches in all literature is the plea addressed by Judah to Joseph to let Benjamin return with his brothers to their father Jacob, and not to insist upon

24

keeping him in Egypt. Long before, Joseph had been sold by his envious brothers to some wandering Ishmaelites, who had carried him down into Egypt. But now he was a great man in Egypt, and as there was a famine in Palestine, his brothers, who had no idea who he was, had to come to him to buy food. Now he proposes to keep their youngest brother with him in Egypt. Judah knows this will break his old father's heart, and his appeal is a real piece of ancient eloquence. It is in Gen., ch. 44. With it should be read ch. 45, which contains Joseph's answer. Together they make one of the great dramatic scenes in literature, as Joseph makes himself known to his brothers.

Hebrew eloquence breaks like a flood, however, in The Book of Deuteronomy. The great feature of it is the address of Moses to the people as they stand at last, after forty years of wandering, on the borders of the Promised Land. It occupies chs. 5 to 26, and after reciting the Ten Commandments and relating the giving of the law, chs. 5 to 11, it goes on in chs. 12 to 26 to set forth a reorganization of Hebrew law, on a higher and more humane plane than before. Chapters 1 to 4 form an introductory address, reviewing the desert wandering just past, and ch. 28 is devoted to listing the hideous, almost unimaginable, curses that will befall the people if they disobey the law. In chs. 29 and 30 Moses solemnly binds the people to keep the divine agreement. The great main oration really reflects the progress of Hebrew legislation toward the close of the seventh century, for it is almost certainly that Book of the Law found in the course of repairing the Temple in the time of Josiah, 621 B.C., and immediately adopted as the law of the land, as so vividly related in II Kings, chs. 22 and 23. One of its striking innovations was the centralization of the Passover celebration in Jerusalem itself; nowhere else could it be observed.

Joshua, like Moses, utters a solemn farewell first to the leaders and then to the people, at the end of his work, Joshua chs. 23 and 24. The Book of Judges also contains one example of ancient oratory, in ch. 9, when Jotham, the youngest son of Jerubbaal, is fleeing for his life from his bloodthirsty brother Abimelech and stops on the top of Mount Gerizim, which looks down upon the town of Shechem, to shout his taunts back at the people of Shechem, where Abimelech had just made himself king. It was this speech that began with one of the few fables in the Bible, the fable of the Trees Electing a King, Judg. 9:8–15. The speech is full of bitter irony and menace and tells its own story.

Samuel's coronation address when he anointed Saul king of Israel is found in I Sam., ch. 12. But much more moving is the speech of Nabal's wife Abigail when she appeals to David not to take vengeance upon her husband, but to keep a clear conscience, I Sam., ch. 25. David's farewell to Solomon, in I Kings, ch. 2, can hardly be called an oration, but it possesses a sinister significance that is highly oriental. The response of the Queen of Sheba to Solomon's reception of her is a marvel of felicity; she certainly rose to the occasion, I Kings 10:6–9:

"The report which I heard in my own land of your affairs and your wisdom was true; but I would not believe the words until I came and saw with my own eyes, and behold, the half was not told me; you surpass in wisdom and prosperity the report which I heard."

The speech of the Prophet Ahijah instigating Jeroboam to rebel and divide Israel into two smaller states is a striking example of a prophet mixing in politics, I Kings 11:26–40; Ahijah lived to rue that day, as he admitted afterwards when Jeroboam's wife came to consult him about her dying child, I Kings 14:1–20.

A very dramatic address from those early times is the Assyrian field marshal's appeal to the population of Jerusalem, gathered upon its walls, not to listen to King Hezekiah but to surrender the city to the Assyrians, in II Kings 18:28–35, which owes much more to Hebrew than to Assyrian rhetoric.

The poet-orators of Judaism, that long line of prophets from Amos, Hosea, Micah, and Isaiah in the eighth century before Christ, on to Malachi, Obadiah, and Joel in the fifth, we may pass over, to be taken up later as part of the great stream of Hebrew poetry, prophetic, priestly, and philosophical. They were beyond question the great contribution of the ancient Hebrew genius to the thought of mankind. It is enough to observe that the literary categories familiar to us from Greek and Latin models do not retain their definite characters when we enter the realm of Hebrew literature. Sermons may be poems, laws may be orations, and philosophies orations and poems at the same time. Only an occasional paragraph of prose can be found among the utterances of Amos, Hosea, and Isaiah, the early literary prophets who preached in the eighth century before Christ; though not even one, in the work of their peasant contemporary Micah.

Yet some prophets did preach in prose.

JEREMIAH

Jeremiah, whose long career of forty years as a prophet, from 627 to 586 B.C., covered the decline and fall of the

Kingdom of Judah, made good use of prose side by side with his poetry, from the very beginning of his work, ch. 1. His rebuke of the apostasy of Judah, ch. 3, and of his people's idolatry, chs. 7 and 8, and unfaithfulness, ch. 11, his Parables of the Waistcloth and the Jars, ch. 13; of the Potter, ch. 18; the Broken Flask, ch. 19; and the Figs, ch. 24; his address on the sanctity of the Sabbath, ch. 17; his warning to King Zedekiah, ch. 21; to Judah, ch. 25; and against the false prophets, ch. 23:30–40; his address on the Cup of Wrath, ch. 25; and on the Yoke of Babylon, ch. 27; and above all the oracle on the New Agreement, ch. 31:27–34; are examples of Jeremiah's prose preaching. It was this last, as quoted in the Epistle to the Hebrews in the New Testament, that actually suggested the names of the New Testament and the Old; it was from Jeremiah that those names were taken. Chapters 32 to 44 and 51:59 to 52:34 are prose, being either narratives about Jeremiah and the collapse of Judah, or utterances of his, connected with the national disaster. Certainly no ancient city's downfall was ever more agonizingly depicted from within than was Jerusalem's in the pages of the high-minded, patriotic, sensitive poet Jeremiah.

Almost half of Jeremiah is prose, but it is so interwoven with his poetical utterances that they can hardly be separated. The prose often gives the background and the setting for the poetry, and it is best to read the whole book as a unit, prose and poetry. It was probably Jeremiah's redoubtable secretary Baruch who edited his work and became in some measure his biographer. The result is, the understanding of The Book of Jeremiah is greatly facilitated, as we read the poetry in the light of the situations and developments embodied in the prose. The Hebrews did not think a book had to be either poetry or prose; they realized that both forms of expression could be advantageously blended in a single volume, especially in dealing with a prophet with the special gifts of Jeremiah.

EZEKIEL

Almost alone among the literary prophets, Ezekiel spoke and wrote principally in prose. His only colleague in this class was Haggai. Ezekiel was a prophet of the Exile. Certainly all his speeches are described as uttered by him while he was in captivity in Babylonia, in the course of the twenty-five years from 592 to 567 B.C. He was originally a priest and at the first capture of Jerusalem, in 597 B.C., he was carried off into exile, and found himself on the banks of the Grand Canal in Babylonia, the Brook or River Chebar. "In the thirtieth year," the book begins, probably meaning Ezekiel's thirtieth year, he had his great vision of the glory of God and felt himself called to prophesy to his dislocated and disheartened countrymen. This vision is the subject of Michelangelo's great picture, the "Vision of Ezekiel." Ezekiel's sermons are full of visions, allegories, and symbols. Here was a man who was both priest and prophet. He had the very difficult duty of keeping his people true to their faith in the face of the greatest discouragements—the destruction of their nation and their worship, and apparently of their religion. The prophet knew how hopeless it was. "They will not listen to you," his voices told him, "for they will not listen to me. . . . But I will make you as hard-faced and stubborn as they; I will make you like adamant, harder than flint." (Ezek. 3: 7, 8.)

Ezekiel was remarkable for his allegories—the Worthless

Vine, ch. 15; the Faithless Wife, ch. 16; the Eagles and the
Vine, ch. 17; the Two Sisters, ch. 23; the Rusty Pot, ch. 24;
the Two Sticks, ch. 37—and his visions, the Glory of God,
ch. 1; Idolatry in Jerusalem, chs. 8 and 9; and most famous
of them all, the Valley of the Dry Bones, ch. 37. Ezekiel
thought of himself as a watchman responsible for the lives of
his people, ch. 3. He worked out the principle of personal re-
sponsibility, ch. 18.

The Book of Ezekiel is for the most part a series of sermons by him. The picture in it is the prophet in his house
(8:1; 14:1; 20:1), surrounded by the elders of the Jewish
community—the beginning of the synagogue meeting of later
Judaism—and addressing to them the messages that came to
him by "the word of the Lord," about Judah's past, about
contemporaneous events, and about future hopes and plans. In
this way, Judah's religion, which had been centered in the
Temple in Jerusalem, was enabled to survive the destruction
of Jerusalem and the Temple, and to find new local centers
that have outlived all the subsequent vicissitudes of Judaism.
To their establishment the eloquence and devotion of Ezekiel
greatly contributed.

Ezekiel hoped for a new Temple, so planned and built
that idolatry could never enter it, and he proposed the plans
for such a Temple and its worship in chs. 40 to 46. But that
can hardly have been an address; it reads more like a written
message left to guide his successors in after days.

HAGGAI

It was on the twenty-eighth of September in the year
520 B.C. that a prophet named Haggai stood up in Jerusalem and

called upon the Jews to rebuild the Temple. Eighteen years had passed since Cyrus the Persian had ended their exile in Babylon and given them free permission to return home. Some of them had done so and busied themselves rebuilding their ruined houses. A new caravan of returning exiles had just arrived from Babylon, and Haggai felt that the time had come to rebuild the Temple, and in response to his stirring challenge the work was undertaken. Two months went by, and the rising structure seemed a small and poor affair beside the memories of Solomon's Temple, which some of them were old enough to recall, and when some belittled the undertaking, Haggai preached again, predicting its future splendor. Two months later Haggai preached twice more, hailing the dawn of a new day for his people, with the Temple going up, and the ritual of his religion at last revived. These four sermons of Haggai on the rebuilding of the Temple in Jerusalem thus fall within four months, from late in September, 520 B.C., to the end of January, 519 B.C. They constitute The Book of Haggai, one of the few prophets who expressed himself entirely in prose.

JESUS

The preaching of Jesus was not poetry, like that of most of the literary prophets, but direct exhortation, affirmation, and parable. The chief examples of it are found in Matthew's series of six great sermons, beginning with the Sermon on the Mount, chs. 5 to 7. The others are chs. 10; 13; 18; 23; and 24–25.

The variety, simplicity, and directness of these sermons give them amazing power. When clothed in the language of today they will strike to the heart of man's chief problems of attitude and conduct.

Jesus' use of parables, a form of fiction, will be considered with other uses of fiction in the Bible. Mark, Matthew, and Luke all show abundant use of them, and they were evidently a favorite form of teaching with Jesus. The extraordinary thing about Jesus' preaching is that, while his standards are so high and his words cut so deep, they do not repel or discourage, but encourage and attract. Beyond any other teacher, he succeeded in making goodness winning and attractive.

There are no parables in John, and Jesus' ideas and teachings have evidently passed into the mind of the Greek author and been reclothed in his own words. Yet they exhibit the extended influence of Jesus' preaching, in the work of one who felt that he had the mind of Christ. The most sustained discourse here is that addressed to the disciples in the Upper Room, chs. 14 to 16, which is certainly one of the great classics of religious devotion.

SERMONS IN THE ACTS

The second volume of Luke's history, known to us as The Acts of the Apostles, contains a series of early Christian speeches, which are not all sermons, for they are uttered in a variety of critical situations. Peter's address to the crowd in Jerusalem on the Day of Pentecost, the harvest festival, Acts, ch. 2, declaring that Jesus is the Messiah of Jewish expectation, is the first of these. Other public addresses of Peter's appear in 3:12–26 and 4:8–12. Stephen's defense before the council is a longer piece of early Christian eloquence, ch. 7.

Peter's speeches in chs. 10 and 11, especially 10:34 to 11:18, complete the series of his addresses in The Acts.

Paul now comes forward as the chief speaker in The Acts, addressing a wide variety of situations. In Acts 13:15–41 he preaches in the synagogue at Antioch. In ch. 17, he addresses the council of the Areopagus, in Athens, in a short speech of extraordinary simplicity and beauty. In ch. 20:17–38 he bids the elders of Ephesus farewell. In ch. 22 he speaks to the Jewish mob from the steps of the Roman barracks in Jerusalem. In ch. 24:9–21 he defends himself before Felix the Governor in Cæsarea. In ch. 26 he makes his great defense before King Agrippa. Two other brief speeches by Paul appear in The Acts, one on the storm-tossed ship somewhere in the Mediterranean, 27:21–26, and one before the leading Jews of Rome, 28:17–20, but even these are finished literary compositions.

It is plain that Luke, like the Greek historians, enlivened his narrative with speeches by the main participants in its action. For Paul's speech, Luke may well have had some information from Paul himself.

II CORINTHIANS

Paul's great defense of himself and of his conduct in the face of the criticisms of his Corinthian converts, in II Corinthians, chs. 10 to 13, is part of a letter but is so personal and vivid as to be virtually a direct address. Its dramatic quality is unsurpassed. Paul speaks as if he were standing before them, throwing back their charges and stating his case. It is more a piece of oratory than a discourse or exposition.

It should be read from that point of view. It forms an interesting contrast to Paul's speeches as given in The Acts.

GALATIANS

Hardly less vigorous and convincing as Pauline oratory is the letter to the Galatians. Little more than fifteen minutes long, it is a perfect blaze of indignant eloquence from the first word to the last. It is a veritable kaleidoscope of great ideas, not the least of them being Paul's belief that in religion, at least in the Christian religion, slaves and women had the same rights as men. This was the society Paul was working night and day to establish, and this was the beginning of liberty and democracy, and the emancipation of women.

HEBREWS

Another great piece of early Christian eloquence is the Epistle to the Hebrews, which is a letter cast in the form of a sermon, since it would be read to the Roman congregation at a meeting of the church. This is the most finished and conscious eloquence in the New Testament. The eleventh chapter, on the heroes of faith, which reaches a noble climax in ch. 12:1 and 2, is a familiar example of its rhetoric. But the whole epistle can be read aloud in three-quarters of an hour.

JAMES

A fine example of the early Christian sermon at its best may be found in the Epistle of James. It is written in the easy, familiar style of the Greek diatribe, but with a finished

Greek vocabulary. Instead of dealing with some single subject, like an ancient literary epistle, it touches a great variety
of phases of Christian conduct, with the utmost vigor and
pungency. It has no single theme, unless it be Christian behavior or the Christian life. The preacher's purpose evidently
was to offer a discourse so varied that everyone in his audience
would be reached by something or other that he said. The
result is, the little sermon, fifteen or twenty minutes long,
reveals no clear course of thought, but a miscellaneous body
of moral instructions of such range and point that the epistle
still seems to many the most practical book in the New Testament.

James has a very modern sound. Cant and sham were
already threatening the churches, and worldliness, partiality,
self-aggrandizement, and gossip must be rebuked. There
is little about doctrine in James, or about Christ, weaknesses
that Luther could not overlook. But it is a ringing statement
of how the Christian is to live and act that is just as apropos
today.

The address, "to the twelve tribes that are scattered over
the world" reflects the belief, as old as Paul, that the Christians are the true Israel, the people of God, and is a way of
presenting the little sermon to Christians everywhere, in
short, of publishing it.

Read James at a sitting, and consider its picture of life in
the Early Church, about the year 100, as compared with life
as you know it in the churches today.

CHAPTER FOUR

The Outline of History

I. HUMAN ORIGINS AND THE BIRTH OF THE NATION

THE FIRST twelve books of the Bible form a historical sequence unique in antiquity. They were written by various hands, working chiefly in the seventh, sixth, and fifth centuries before Christ, but standing together they form the most coherent, continuous account of human origins, and of one ancient people's history as it understood it, that has come down to us from the ancient world. It is man's first attempt to organize his knowledge of his past into what we would call an outline of history.

Herodotus has been called the father of history, but his great work, after two or three legendary pages, starts in with 560 B.C. But the last event recorded in II Kings was the release of King Jehoiachin from prison in 561 B.C., the year before the accession of Crœsus, with which Herodotus' main narrative begins. We may almost say that chronologically speaking Herodotus begins where II Kings leaves off.

Although these twelve books from Genesis to II Kings form a fairly continuous series, one beginning where the preceding one ends, they fall into three groups: (1) the Penta-

36

teuch, Genesis to Deuteronomy; (2) Joshua, Judges, and
Ruth; and (3) the books of Samuel and Kings.

THE PENTATEUCH

There is to begin with, the Pentateuch, or "five-volume"
work, Genesis to Deuteronomy, which has so entranced the
religious imagination. It covers the origin and laws of the
Hebrews. In Hebrew it forms a single huge scroll, forty or
fifty feet in length and correspondingly difficult to handle
and consult. To be able to find any given place in this mass
of unchaptered columns was one of the feats upon which the
ancient Jewish scribe prided himself. It is in this form that
the Pentateuch still lies in the ark at the back of the platform
in modern synagogues of the better class. When the Greeks
put these writings into their language, they divided it into
five rolls of practical size, each twenty or twenty-five feet
long, and gave the five parts the Greek names by which we
know them: Genesis, the beginning; Exodus, the emigration;
Leviticus, the Levites' book; Arithmoi, which we translate
Numbers; and Deuteronomy, the second giving of the Law.
The Greeks called those five books the Pentateuch, or five
volumes, but the Jews called them simply the Law, or the
book of Moses, since he was its dominant character—emancipator, lawgiver, and prophet.

It must be remembered that the literature of Western
Asia was anonymous; the few Hebrew literary prophets whose
names we know were exceptions to what was undoubtedly the
rule. The Semites did not think of authorship as an individual
matter as the Greeks did. Literature was to them a social
product. What a man wrote he had largely absorbed from his

fellow men, of whom he was simply the mouthpiece. It is not strange, therefore, that we cannot name the author of one of these twelve books. They make no effort to indicate their authorship. They come to us rather as woven out of the utterances of many men. Priests and prophets both worked upon them, through centuries of development and change.

This is especially true of the Pentateuch. Its oldest book, Deuteronomy, is the mysterious roll of the Law found lying about in the Temple when it was being restored in King Josiah's reformation, in 621 B.C., after its long neglect under his half-heathen predecessors Manasseh and Amon. It had been written in secret by some fugitive prophet in the times when the prophets' voices were silenced, and left behind him in the hope that it might some day lead to the restoration of Israel's religion and a more spiritual and moral Temple worship. It is cast in the form of a great oration addressed by Moses to the Hebrew people, when after forty years of wandering they at last approached the Promised Land.

About this great expression of the Hebrew faith there gathered eventually the great mass of history, law, and tradition that now precedes it. Many sources entered into it; foreign influences contributed to it; its stories of the Creation and the Flood have some parallels in Babylonian tablets, and many of its laws appear in the old Babylonian code of Hammurabi. But out of all these the Hebrew religious genius finally shaped one great narrative, attempting the gigantic task of organizing all their history, law, and tradition into a great coherent whole, which should embody their beliefs about the origin of the world and man, the dawn of conscience and the sense of God, the rise of races, nations, tribes, and families, their own in particular; its founders, Abraham and his grandson Jacob, or Israel; his twelve sons, each the founder of the tribe that bore his name; especially Joseph, whose stirring and romantic story concludes the book of Genesis, chs. 37 to 50.

The form in which the writer of Genesis cast his religious ideas is so bold and crude that the reader is often bewildered by it. How well Erasmus, in 1515, put the problem and solved it:

"If in the Old Testament you see nothing but history, and read that Adam was made out of mud, that his wife was unobtrusively taken from his side while he slept; that the serpent tempted her with forbidden fruit; that God walked in the cool of the evening; and that a guard was placed at the gates of Paradise to keep the fugitives from returning— would you not fancy the whole thing a fable from Homer's workshop? But under those wrappings, . . . Good Heavens! What splendid wisdom lies concealed!"

Genesis is a great encyclopedia of Hebrew thought, and its solutions of the great problems that confront the human mind. Its great achievement was that it unified it all, moral and material, as the work of one supreme being, who was creator of both body and spirit, whose will was the moral law, but who was ready to forgive man's moral failures. If we compare it with Homer or Herodotus, it exhibits a deeper moral earnestness and spiritual insight than they.

Genesis can be read aloud in three hours and a half; it can be easily read in an afternoon or an evening; read to oneself, as we say, it will take only about half that long. It is a great tribute to the slow motion imparted to it by the old chapter and verse divisions that it looks to most people like a month's work!

This is partly due, of course, to the extraordinary wealth of interest and suggestion with which it is filled. Since it offers so much food for thought, it may be broken into four chapters, more rational than the fifty into which Stephen Langton broke it seven hundred and fifty years ago:

I. The Story of Mankind, from the creation to the rise of the nations, chs. I to II.

II. The Story of Abraham, with especial reference to his religious experience, 12:1 to 25:18.

III. The Story of Jacob, his domestic and his inner life, 25:19 to 37:1.

IV. The Romance of Joseph, the slave boy who became a statesman, 37:2 to 50:26.

Genesis is not hard reading in any version, for it is almost entirely narrative; indeed, it reveals the oriental story-teller at his best and offers the most convincing picture of ancient patriarchal life to be found anywhere. A good modern speech translation will save you from the slow-down that the antique diction always causes the reader and will give you a much more vivid picture of what Genesis has to offer.

The second of the five books into which the practical Greeks divided the Pentateuch is Exodus, the emigration. It is not so long as Genesis and can be read aloud in less than three hours, or to oneself in half that time. Its hero is Moses. The book falls into two parts:

I. The oppression of the Israelites in Egypt and their escape under the leadership of Moses, chs. I to 18.

II. The sojourn at Sinai, and the giving of the Law, chs. 19 to 40. This legislation includes some very primitive elements, such as the Book of the Covenant, chs. 20:22 to 23:33, which perpetuates old legal practices taken over from the Canaanites after the conquest, and the still older little book of the covenant, in ch. 34, which may be regarded as the germ of the whole Hebrew legislation.

The most enduring part of the Law is what we know as the Ten Commandments, ch. 20:2–17. They form the prelude to the Exodus legislation, which went on from moral injunctions to the arrangements for the building and furnishing of the Tabernacle, a portable sanctuary which the Hebrews were to make and carry with them in the wanderings that followed.

The remaining books of the Pentateuch, Leviticus, Numbers, and Deuteronomy, like the last twenty-two chapters of Exodus, consist almost entirely of Hebrew laws. Leviticus means the Levitical book, that is, the book of instructions for the priests and their assistants, the Levites. Levi was the priestly tribe; its men were set apart for the priesthood. Leviticus presents the law of sacrifice, telling just how victims were to be offered; it tells how priests were to be installed and gives the laws defining ceremonial uncleanness and holiness.

Numbers, so called because it begins with the census taken at Sinai, presents a variety of laws, interspersed with narratives—the journey from Sinai to the borders of Canaan, the sending of scouts into Canaan, collisions with border tribes, Amorites and Moabites, with their prophet Balaam. These narratives bring the Israelites to the land of Moab, east of the Jordan, at Jericho.

Then Deuteronomy sums up the laws in the form of a farewell oration addressed by Moses to the Israelites on the threshold of the Promised Land. It is represented as his great valedictory. Its oratorical possibilities were thoroughly proved half a century ago, when Richard Green Moulton would hold his lecture audiences all over the East and Middle West literally spellbound as he recited the whole oration.

All these books must be read as the legal inheritance of Judaism, to be compared with the famous code of Hammurabi, king of Babylon about 1800 B.C., which was discovered at Susa in December and January, 1901–1902, and the Ras Shamra tablets found near the site of Antioch in 1929. But these legal materials are so intricate and varied that they call for special treatment in Chapter Five as laws.

The Outline of History

II. HEBREW LAW

For the Jews, the characteristic part of their Scriptures was the Law, or Instruction, the Torah, as they called it. They found it in the first five books of the Old Testament, which the Greeks called the Pentateuch, but the Jews knew it as Moses, or the Law of Moses.

The legal parts of it comprised Exodus, chs. 19 to 40, all of Leviticus, most of Numbers, except chs. 22 to 24, and all of Deuteronomy. It is far from being a systematic legal statement, however, mingling various stages of primitive legislation with more fully organized systems of laws. When the Hebrews wished to improve their code, and propounded a new one, they still preserved the old ones, and eventually put them back into their law book. This enables us to see the Hebrew Law in its successive stages and to observe its development.

Much light is also thrown upon the complex problem of the development of the Hebrew law by the discovery in 1901–1902 of the laws of Hammurabi, king of Babylonia at least eighteen hundred years before Christ, which often parallel the Hebrew laws of the Pentateuch. Hammurabi declared that these laws were revealed by the sun god Shamash, very much as the Hebrew lawgivers regarded their laws as divinely given. It was one way of expressing the recognition that law and order were divine gifts and divine demands. The mass of cuneiform and other tablets found at Ras Shamra, on the outskirts of ancient Antioch, in 1929 and after, throws much light on the laws of the land about 1400 B.C., some two centuries before the Hebrews entered Canaan. The points at which the Hebrew legislation corrected or reversed the laws previously in force there are especially instructive.

If you have a legal mind and are interested in ancient legislation, seven different legal codes may be distinguished in the Pentateuch. It is instructive to read them one by one and observe the stage of social and moral progress that each reflects.

1. One of the oldest of these was observed by Goethe in Ex. 34:10–26, the so-called Little Book of the Covenant, and discussed in an article he published in 1773. It is chiefly a ritual, containing five laws about festivals and five about sacrifice. It is very old, and was probably taken over from the Canaanites as early as 1200 B.C., when the Hebrews invaded Palestine and settled there.

2. Another code, probably just as old, and also of Canaanite origin, is found in Ex. 20:22 to 23:33, the Book of the Covenant. It too was of Canaanite origin; indeed, most of it can be found, in Babylonian, in the Hammurabi code and was doubtless the law of the land when the Hebrews entered Canaan and became a settled people. They naturally adopted the agricultural and other practices of the population which they gradually dispossessed. In the Hammurabi code the laws of property (Ex. 21:33 to 22:15) come before the laws about persons (Ex. 21:2–32), but this order is reversed in the Book

of the Covenant, which reflects a higher regard for persons than the Babylonian code had.

3. A third code, the most famous of all, is the Ten Commandments. They appear twice in the Pentateuch, in Ex. 20:2–17 and in Deut. 5:6–21. The Exodus list is probably the earlier form of it, for it places the wife second on the list of property, and explains the Sabbath as commemorating God's rest after the six days of creation. The Deuteronomy list, on the other hand, puts the wife first among the possessions not to be coveted and explains the Sabbath as designed to give a man's family and even his slaves a chance to rest. This is more like the prophet's point of view; the Exodus form is more priestly in spirit. It is the form given in the Catechism in *The Book of Common Prayer.*

4. With the fourth code we come into clearer light, for it is what we know as the book of Deuteronomy, at least chs. 5 to 26, and 28. This, or the most of it, is the Book of Law found in the Temple when it was being repaired and restored in Josiah's time, 621 B.C., as so vividly described in II Kings, chs. 22 and 23. It was written by some forgotten prophet probably in hiding during the perilous times of Manasseh, 692–639 B.C., and sought to bring together the two main streams of Hebrew religion, prophetic and priestly, in a legislation that would do full justice to both. Chapters 5:22 to 11:32 are retrospect and admonition; 5:1–21 and chs. 12 to 26 are laws. The religious ceremonial was to carry with it high ideals of personal uprightness and of social justice. But no sacrifice was to be offered except in the Temple in Jerusalem, and only in Jerusalem could their great annual festival, the Passover, be observed. Read 5:1–21 and chs. 12 to 26, which constitute a reorganization of previously existing

laws, including the Book of the Covenant (code 2 above), on a higher plane than before.

EZEKIEL

The closing chapters of Ezekiel describe his visions of the Temple of the future and the worship that was to go on in it, chs. 40 to 46. They constitute a design for a Temple legislation, from 572 B.C., and though they never actually became a part of Jewish law, they had a strong influence upon the second Temple when it came to be built, in 520 B.C., and upon the form of its worship. Ezekiel was in exile with the most of his people in Babylonia, and Solomon's Temple had been destroyed and its worship had ceased. He believed that this disaster had come about because the people had failed to maintain the holiness God demanded of them, and he dreamed of a day when the Temple should be rebuilt and the worship of God resumed in it with a sanctity that would prevent the recurrence of any such calamity.

Ezekiel's conception of the significance of holiness in the relation between God and his people was an important element in the holiness code that so soon followed.

5. A fifth legislation is found chiefly in Lev., chs. 17 to 26. It owes much to the work of Ezekiel. It is the holiness code, so called because of its emphasis upon holiness as the great bond between God and his people. The priests in particular were to observe the strictest rules. It repeats many old laws, but lays great stress on their observance as a means of raising the nation, especially the priesthood, to a level of ceremonial and moral holiness that would unite them with their holy God. In form it is another address by Moses, but

a number of traits (its use of Jeremiah and consciousness of the destruction of Jerusalem) show that it was written in the midst of the Exile, about 550 B.C. It deals chiefly with the slaughtering of animals, marriage, the priesthood, the festivals, and the sabbatical year.

6. Fifty or seventy-five years later the holiness code was expanded into a sixth code, the priestly legislation. It reflects the practices of the new Temple which the Jews, now freed from captivity (538 B.C.), have erected in Jerusalem. Their ruler is no earthly king, but God himself. They needed no secular legislation, for the Persian Empire of which they were subjects took care of that. Judaism now becomes practically the Jewish Church. Religious laws become more rigid and religion more formal. The Jewish religion is now transformed into the legalistic observance of a mass of regulations. This is preserved chiefly in Leviticus, chs. 1 to 27, though portions of it can be found also in Exodus and Numbers. With it arose also the wonderful series of teachings by story—the origin of the Sabbath, Gen. 1:1 to 2:3; the story of the Flood, chs. 6 to 9; God's covenant with Abraham, ch. 17; and many more.

7. Finally, about 400 B.C. some great Hebrew genius brought together his people's long heritage of law and tradition, ancient and modern, casting it all into one great narrative. It was one unbroken story, from the institution of the Sabbath at the creation down through the rise of nations and civilization to the giving of the Hebrew Law, through Moses the one and only lawgiver, whose death, in the last chapter, Deut. 34, showed that the Law stood finished and complete, never to be enlarged. We know it as five books, Genesis to Deuteronomy, but the Jews called it the Law, the Torah, and came to think of it as really the complete expression of the

will of God. Into it were wrought the old codes as well as the new, for they had never destroyed them. Even the Ten Commandments were repeated. And the whole legislation, which began with Ex., ch. 20, was now preceded by a narrative telling the story of man and especially the Hebrew people, from their remotest ancestor down to their bondage in Egypt, their emancipation by Moses, and their journey to Mount Sinai, where amidst the grandeur of its scenery the Law was to be revealed. It was an ancient outline of history written from a deeply religious point of view.

To the modern reader the narrative of Genesis 1 to Exodus 19 is of far greater interest than most of the legal provisions that follow. For here is an ancient account of the origin of man and of his characteristic institutions—the family, the tribe, the city, the nation, language, administration, religion—that evinces an extraordinary power of insight and reflection. Through it all shines, though sometimes dimly, the deep conviction that man is made for goodness, and that that is in fact the will of God. The ancient world that shows through the story is a crude and brutal one, indeed, and so it was, but there is also visible a deep tendency toward better moral standards which the writers find based in the constitution of man and in the will of God. There is a moral universe. Conscience is the voice of the Creator. The development of character is what gives meaning to life.

CHAPTER SIX

The Outline of History

III. THE CONQUEST AND THE KINGDOM

THE LAST page of Deuteronomy tells how Moses from Mount Pisgah looked westward across the Jordan at the Promised Land, and then died and was buried in the land of Moab, Deut. 34:1–6. He had found a home for his people, but it remained for them to make it theirs. This was the task of his successor, Joshua.

So with The Book of Joshua we return from the masses of laws that make up the bulk of Exodus, Leviticus, Numbers, and Deuteronomy, to the great narrative of the history of the Hebrew people continued in the seven books from Joshua to II Kings.

These fall into two parts: Joshua, Judges, and Ruth deal with the conquest and settlement of Canaan, while the books of Samuel and Kings tell the story of the Hebrew monarchy, its rise and fall.

THE BOOK OF JOSHUA

Upon the death of Moses, the leadership of the Hebrews passed to his able lieutenant, Joshua. The Book of Joshua is the legendary story of the conquest of Canaan. The Jordan stops its flow to let the people cross dry-shod, and the walls of

49

Jericho, the first stronghold in their path, fall down without a blow, chs. 1 to 6. The city of Ai offered a stout resistance but was taken by a stratagem, chs. 7 and 8. Joshua fought on against the kings of the Amorites, who besieged his allies in the town of Gibeon; Joshua made a night march to its relief, surprised the Amorites and won a great victory. It was then that in the heat of pursuit he cried out to the sun and moon to stand still, chs. 9 and 10. Other battles and victories followed, chs. 11 and 12.

The rest of the book deals with the allotment of the conquered lands among the tribes, chs. 13 to 22, and Joshua's farewell and death, chs. 23 and 24.

THE BOOK OF JUDGES

The conquest was very incomplete, however, and for many years there was fighting in one place or another to establish the Israelites in their possession of Canaan. In the course of it a series of champions arose who led local groups to victory here and there over the land. This is The Book of Judges. One of the first of these leaders was Barak, chapters 4 and 5. He was aided in his campaign by two women, Jael, who killed the Canaanite general Sisera when after the battle he sought refuge in her tent, and Deborah, the prophetess, whose war song celebrating the victory is probably the oldest poem of its length in the Bible, about 1150 B.C. She taunts the tribes that sent no contingents to the battle:

> "In the clans of Reuben great were the debates. . . .
> Gilead remaining beyond the Jordan; . . .
> Asher stayed by the sea-coast,
> And remained by his creeks.
> "Zebulun was a people who exposed themselves to death,
> And Naphtali, on the heights of the field." (Judg. 5:16–18.)

Gideon with his ingenious and original tactics subdued the Midianites, chs. 6 to 8; Jephthah, whose tragic sacrifice of his daughter we know so well, was the conqueror of the Ammonites, chs. 10 to 12; Samson was the champion against the Philistines, though he fell a victim to their wiles, chs. 13 to 16. The strange stories of Micah and the Danites, chs. 17 and 18, and Gibeah and the Benjaminites, chs. 19 to 21, conclude this book of wild, fierce tales of guile and lust and blood, hardly matched in their kind in all the world.

THE BOOK OF RUTH

The little idyl of Ruth follows The Book of Judges in the Bible, only because its story falls in the days of the Judges. But it belongs to Israel's fiction, rather than to its history, and should be read among its tales and stories.

I AND II SAMUEL

The narrative emerges into clearer light as we enter the final group of books in the great historical sequence—the books of Samuel and Kings. The Greeks called these books Reigns, and numbered them I, II, III, and IV, and indeed the Hebrew kingdom does make its appearance in the first of them, which we know as I Samuel. Samuel is the leading figure for a time, it is true; he becomes the last of the judges and chooses and anoints the first king of Israel, Saul, the valiant captain, but lives to regret his choice, chs. 1 to 15. Read them for the story of the work of Samuel and the founding of the kingdom. Then, though in fear of his life, Samuel goes to Bethlehem and anoints a new king, a mere shepherd boy named David, the youngest of eight brothers. The bold exploits of this young man, down to the death of Saul, fill the rest of I Samuel, chs. 16 to 31, which with II Samuel might almost be called the Book of David. It should be read as a unit, for its epic picture of David the fugitive, the bandit chief, the refugee among the Philistines. These were the tales dear to the Jewish heart that made David ever after the national hero.

II Samuel begins with David's vengeance for the death of Saul. He has to fight Saul's forces for the throne but wins it and becomes king. By a mysterious strategem he takes Jerusalem from the Jebusites and makes it his capital, instead of Hebron. He brings the Ark, the symbol of God's presence, to Jerusalem, and checks his enemies on every side—Philistines, Moabites, Syrians, Ammonites, chs. 1 to 10. But his passion for Bathsheba and his domestic troubles, especially with his son Absalom who revolted against him, show him degenerating into a typical oriental monarch, chs. 11 to 24. The last scene is David's vainglorious taking of a census of Israel, to atone for which he bought the threshing floor of Araunah the Jebusite and built an altar on it. This later gave place to the great altar of burnt offering in Solomon's Temple and the spot is now covered by the dome of the Mosque of Omar, the chief landmark of modern Jerusalem.

Read chs. 1 to 10 for the successes of David, and chs. 11 to 24 chiefly for his mistakes and failures.

I AND II KINGS

I Kings takes up the narrative without a hitch. David on his deathbed makes Bathsheba's son Solomon his successor.

Chapters 1 to 11 record Solomon's reign—his ruthless beginning, his wisdom, his building of the Temple and dedication of it, his wide interests, his foreign wives and the shrines he built for their gods. His reign of forty years was the golden age of Israel, but as soon as he was dead, Jeroboam, his old commissioner of labor, stirred the ten northern tribes to revolt and form a kingdom of their own with its capital at Shechem and its sanctuaries at Dan and Bethel. This was the disruption, or division of the kingdom. Thenceforth the Hebrews formed two smaller kingdoms, the northern one being known as Israel and the southern as Judah. So through the rest of the book, chs. 12 to 22, the stories of the two kingdoms go on side by side, the writer reporting each reign, and dating the beginning of a reign in Judah by the regnal year of the king in Israel and vice versa. This makes possible a very substantial chronology of both kingdoms, as long as they endured. The sequence of their reigns and a table of their dates may be found in Chapter Twenty-One of this book, entitled "The Historical Background."

In I Kings, ch. 17, there emerges a figure of more consequence than any of the kings the book describes—Elijah the prophet. He stood forth to condemn the idolatries introduced into Israel with the Phœnician princess Jezebel, whom King Ahab had married. Elijah's towering figure, along with his junior colleague Elisha, dominates the rest of the book, down to the death of his principal adversary, Ahab, king of Israel.

Read chs. 1 to 11 for the accession and reign of Solomon, and chs. 12 to 22 for the account of the revolt of the northern tribes and the history of the two new kingdoms as they go on side by side, Israel in the north and Judah in the south, with the appearance of the Prophet Elijah in the north, and his campaign against Baal worship there.

I and II Kings in ancient Hebrew formed one book, just as I and II Samuel did; it was the Greek translators of the third or second century before Christ who divided each of them into two more convenient rolls. II Kings goes on from the death of Ahab, with the carrying of Elijah up to heaven in a whirlwind, and the wonders wrought by Elisha, chs. 1 to 8. Encouraged by Elisha, Jehu seizes the throne of Israel, and wipes out the family of Ahab and the worshipers of Baal. His dynasty retains the throne for a hundred years, 843 to 744 B.C., but in 722–721 B.C. Israel goes down before the Assyrians under Sargon II, chs. 9 to 17. Every king is judged by the writer as doing that which was right or that which was evil in the sight of the Lord.

The little Kingdom of Judah had still a century of independence, from the days of Hezekiah, when Sennacherib threatened Jerusalem, in Isaiah's times, on through the half-heathen reigns of Manasseh and Amon, and the reformation under Josiah, when The Book of Deuteronomy was found and became the first law book of the Hebrews. In the east Assyria was going down before the new Babylonian Empire; Nineveh fell in 612 B.C., and a few years later, in 597 and 586 B.C., Nebuchadnezzar's armies overwhelmed Judah and finally destroyed Jerusalem, chs. 18 to 25. The last pathetic incident related in II Kings is that in 561 B.C. poor Jehoiachin, the last rightful king of Judah, who became king at eighteen and reigned three months, was released from prison in Babylon and pensioned for the rest of his life. It was the thirty-seventh year of his captivity. (II Kings 25:27–30.)

Read II Kings, chs. 1 to 8, for further stories of Elijah
and Elisha. Then read chs. 9 to 17 for the history of the two
kingdoms from Jehu's usurpation of the throne of Israel to
the destruction of the Northern Kingdom. Finally read chs.
18 to 25 for the further history of Judah and its final overthrow by the Babylonians. A brief sketch of these events will
be found in Chapter Twenty-One, "The Historical Background."

It is hard to realize that only a little more than a century
ago all that we knew of the great ancient empires of Babylonia, Assyria, and Egypt was derived from the Old Testament and Herodotus. It was only after the decipherment of
hieroglyphic and cuneiform that it became possible to supplement their accounts with the records and remains of those
great peoples themselves—their inscriptions, tablets, and
papyri, as well as the records of the Persians who followed
them. The effect of these discoveries has been to roll up the
curtain on the history of these ancient empires. They have
also thrown a great light on the history, literature, and laws
of the Hebrews.

CHAPTER SEVEN

The History Rewritten and Continued

THE GREAT historical and legal sequence that we know as Genesis to II Kings may be thought of as an ancient Jewish encyclopedia, embodying their traditions, beliefs, and laws and tracing their history down to the middle of the Exile in Babylon. For their Babylonian conquerors removed all but the poorest of them from Jerusalem and transferred them to Mesopotamia. The sixty years of this period of Exile were very fruitful in Jewish thought and literature, but the years that followed it were full of discouragement for the few Jews who returned to Palestine.

It was the victory of the Persians under Cyrus the Great over the Babylonians that had brought the Exile to an end, in 538 B.C. But it had left the Jews under new masters, the Persians, and for two hundred years they were subjects of the great king. Then out of the west came the Greeks under Alexander, in 333 B.C., to defeat the Persian army and take Palestine, and the Jews once more changed masters. After two centuries and a half of foreign domination, their priests turned their thoughts from the humiliating present to their ancient glories, and toward 300 B.C. rewrote their history, painting it in stronger colors. So arose a second historical sequence, based on the first, tracing the history from the death of Saul, I Chron., ch. 10, to the coming of Ezra from Persia in 397 B.C., Ezra. chs. 7; 8, and his work of reformation, Ezra, chs. 9; 10. This new series is known to us as Chronicles, Ezra, and Nehemiah.

By that time the Jews were laying great stress on purity of Jewish descent, and genealogical tables were coming to be of great importance among them. It is not strange, therefore, that I Chronicles begins with such tables, which occupy chs. 1 to 8, while ch. 9 gives the roster of the exiles who returned from Babylon, the heads of families, priests, Levites, gate-keepers—even the functionary in charge of the pastry of flat-cakes for the Temple. The modern reader will find little of interest to him in these long lists: "Adam, Seth, Enosh; Kenan, Mahalalel, Jared, Enoch, Methuselah, Lamech; Noah, Shem, Ham, and Japheth," but to the priestly leaders of the woebegone little community in Jerusalem they were of absorbing interest, for they enabled them to trace their ancestry back to Abraham and even to Adam.

The new historians did not concern themselves with Saul, nor the kings of the Northern Kingdom of Israel, but only with David and Solomon and the kings descended from them, who reigned over what they considered the loyal and legitimate Kingdom of Judah. So, while the books of Samuel and Kings are freely used for the history of the kings of Judah, no effort is made in Chronicles to record the names or deeds of the kings of the Northern Kingdom of Israel. In fact, Chronicles has been described as a priestly history of Jerusalem, greatly emphasizing the labors of David and Solomon upon the Temple and everything connected with it.

The narrative begins with the death of Saul, drawn from
I Samuel, ch. 31, to which the writer adds the moral of his
fate, ch. 10. It proceeds with the accession of David, and his
reign, down to the census-taking, all greatly condensed from
II Samuel, but also elaborated from the writer's priestly
point of view. Thus the loyal army that rallied about David
when he came forward to claim the throne numbered 341,600
men. This narrative fills chs. 11 to 21. It is followed by
David's plans for the Temple and its worship, his organization of the Temple staff, his officers of administration and the
turning over of his Temple plans to Solomon for execution,
chs. 22 to 29. Chapter 29 describes his tranquil death. There
is no mention in Chronicles of his base treatment of Uriah in
order to get Bathsheba for himself or of his domestic troubles
with Amnon and Absalom, which form so much of II Samuel.

Read I Chron., chs. 1 to 9, for the genealogies and lists by
which the later Jews traced their ancestries to the patriarchs.
Then read chs. 10 to 21 for the fate of Saul and the reign of
David. Then read chs. 22 to 29 for David's plans for the
Temple and its organization, and then his death.

II Chronicles begins with Solomon's reign, chs. 1 to 9,
with especial emphasis on the building, furnishing, and dedication of the Temple, chs. 2 to 7. Chapters 10 to 20 tell the
story of the reigns from Rehoboam, when the ten tribes of the
north left Judah and broke away to form the Kingdom of
Israel, to Jehoshaphat upon whose piety and prosperity the
Chronicler lays great stress. Chapters 21 to 28 carry the story
on from Jehoram to Ahaz, and chs. 29 to 36 tell of the reformation under Hezekiah, the reaction under Manasseh and
Amon, the Deuteronomic reformation under Josiah, and then

the overthrow of Judah by the Babylonians under Nebuchadnezzar, followed by the exile in Babylon, ending with the release of the Jews from their long captivity of sixty years,
when the Persians under Cyrus wrested the empire from the
Babylonians in 538 B.C. A brief sketch of these events will be
found in the chapter on "The Historical Background," Chapter Twenty-One.

Elijah is barely mentioned in Chronicles (II, 21:12);
Elisha is not mentioned at all. The writer's interest is with the
priests and the Temple; from his interest in the Temple music
and his knowledge of it is evident that he himself was a
Levite and a Temple musician (I Chron. 25:6–8, etc.) in
the second Temple, the one built by the returning exiles after
the captivity was over. The moralizing tendency of the books
of Kings is carried much farther in Chronicles, which height-
ens the whole picture. The bad kings are much worse, the
good kings much better than in the Samuel-Kings narrative.
The armies are much larger, the expenditures greater, the
whole account of the ancient kingdom richer. The period
covered is that of I Sam., ch. 31, to II Kings, ch. 25. But
Chronicles carries the story on twenty-three years farther than
Kings, for while Kings stops with the release of Jehoiachin
from prison in 561 B.C., Chronicles ends with the amnesty
of Cyrus the Persian in 538 B.C. which made it possible for
the Jews to go back to Palestine.

Read II Chronicles, chs. 1 to 9, for the reign of Solomon
and his building of the Temple. Read chs. 10 to 20 for the story
of the kings of Judah, from Rehoboam to Jehoshaphat. Read
chs. 21 to 28 for the history of Judah from Jehoram to
Ahaz, and chs. 29 to 36 for the remaining years of Judah's

existence, until its destruction by Babylon, and sixty years later the conclusion of the Exile through Persia's victory over Babylon.

But the writer of Chronicles did not stop there. He went on in The Book of Ezra to tell of the return, and the rebuilding and dedication of the Temple, chs. 1 to 6. He also embodied in his record a work from the hand of Nehemiah, the cupbearer of Artaxerxes I, who came out to Jerusalem in 444 B.C. and rebuilt its walls. This book, apart from 7:6 to 12:26, which relate to Ezra, is a fascinating piece of autobiography, telling of Nehemiah's sorrow over the wretched condition of Jerusalem, his courageous request for a leave of absence to build its walls, his arrival and nocturnal inspection of the ruined walls, his enlistment of the Jewish residents in a record-breaking rebuilding of them in fifty-two days—a little over seven weeks—and his social reforms. Nehemiah should be read continuously, omitting 7:6 to 12:26. While it is autobiographical in form, being told in the first person singular, that may be merely a literary device, like the famous autobiography of Darius I, preserved in the Behistun inscription and in an Aramaic version. But it is at any rate perhaps the most vivid and realistic glimpse given us in the Old Testament of Jewish life and doings in old Jerusalem.

The Chronicler, as we may call him, placed the work of Ezra before that of Nehemiah, evidently supposing that Ezra came out from Mesopotamia to Palestine under Artaxerxes I, about 458 B.C., not under Artaxerxes II, about 397 B.C., as most scholars now believe. In Ezra, chs. 7 and 8, the historian tells of the expedition of Ezra the scribe, who came to Jerusalem from Babylon with money and reinforcements, and especially with the Law of Moses, which he read to all the people in a great outdoor meeting in Jerusalem, so graphically described in Nehemiah, chs. 8 to 10. A great deal is made of Ezra's efforts to teach the people and especially the heads of families and the priests the contents of this law, which seems to have been unfamiliar to them, and they are finally persuaded to adopt it and bind themselves to its faithful observance. This narrative, Nehemiah 7:6 to 12:26, should be read before Ezra, chs. 9 and 10. Evidently the Law of Moses, that is, the Pentateuch, reached its full stature among the Jews of Babylonia, and was thought of as now for the first time communicated to the smaller Jerusalem colony, in its great public meeting.

It now appeared that the Law as understood by Ezra forbade the Jews to marry outside their own people. But numbers of the Jews in Palestine had married outsiders, and they were now called upon to cast off such wives along with their children. The purpose of this cruel policy was, of course, to safeguard the people against the infiltration of idolatrous practices that these foreign wives might naturally bring with them and teach their children. Yet the Law left room for marriage with alien women; it allowed a Jewish soldier to marry a foreign captive, Deut. 21:10–14. But Ezra insisted that foreign wives must go, and went to great lengths to accomplish this end. Ezra, chs. 9 and 10.

The narratives of Ezra-Nehemiah will be better understood if they are read in the order—Ezra 1 to 6; Neh. 1:1 to 7:5; 12:27 to 13:31; Ezra 7; 8; Neh. 7:6 to 12:26; Ezra 9; 10.

CHAPTER EIGHT

Scattered Poetical Pieces

T O THE reader of the Bible it is a matter of great importance that more than one-third of the Old Testament is poetry—not only books whose titles announce the fact, like The Psalms and the Song of Songs, but most of Isaiah and Jeremiah, and those of equally great but less voluminous poets, from Hosea to Malachi, whom we mistakenly call the Minor Prophets. In fact, the oldest books in the Old Testament, Amos and Hosea, are poetry. And poetry is to be approached and read in a very different way from prose. Prose may at least be taken in a matter-of-fact sense, but this is seldom true of poetry.

Poetry makes an imaginative demand upon the reader; he must yield to the poet's spell and follow him into the realm of the imagination. To refuse to do this, and to treat the poet's flights as matter-of-fact statements would be disastrous in the extreme. The poetry of the Bible must be read as poetry, if it is to be read at all. This is the most familiar distinction in literature, in which poetry and prose are the basic categories, never to be confused, since they reflect different attitudes of mind.

So few versions of the English Bible distinguish its poetry

from its prose that the reader must be on his guard against mistaking one for the other, and treating it all as prose. For one thing, poetry is much more charged with emotion and excitement than prose; it is in general far more intense and filled with feeling. Prose generally supposes a more normal mood on the part of the reader. The reader must remember that not only Job, The Psalms, the Proverbs, the Song of Songs, and Lamentations are poetry, but also most of Isaiah, Jeremiah, Hosea, Joel, Amos, Obadiah, Micah, Nahum, Habakkuk, Zephaniah, and Malachi. As it would be difficult to remember this list, it may be well to take one's Bible and write "Poetry" under the title of each of these books, unless you are using a modern translation in which the poetical books are printed as poetry. If you have a complete Old Version, that is, one with all the contents of the King James Bible of 1611, including the fourteen books of the Apocrypha, along with the Old and New Testaments, you should write "Poetry" under the titles of the Wisdom of Solomon, Ecclesiasticus, The Book of Baruch, the Song of the Three Children, and the Prayer of Manasses. The recognition of this distinction will save the reader much unnecessary perplexity and confusion.

It is at once clear that reading the poetry of the Bible necessarily draws upon the imagination of the reader, just as the reading of Shakespeare or Milton does. The great Robertson once observed that the reading of great poetry demands as much intellectual effort of the reader as the higher mathematics. Yet one-third of the Old Testament is of this kind. We cannot escape the intellectual demand thus made upon the reader, nor save him from it. But we can at least inform him when he is entering this difficult realm, by the familiar device of printing poetry as it should be printed, so that he knows at once that he is no longer reading prose, and at once instinctively makes the mental adjustment required.

Although sixteen books of the Old Testament and five of the Apocrypha are wholly or mainly poetical, a total of twenty-one books out of fifty-three, there is poetry scattered all through most of the other books of the Old Testament and the Apocrypha. In the oldest narratives of Genesis, the curses pronounced after the Fall, upon the serpent, the woman, and the man, are poetical, Gen. 3:13–19. The savage sword-song of Lamech, at the dawn of the bronze age, ch. 4:23, 24, is poetry. Noah's curse upon his grandson Canaan, 9:25–27; Melchizedek's blessing of Abraham, 14:19, 20; Isaac's blessing of Jacob, 27:28, 29; and Jacob's blessing of his sons, ch. 49; are other pieces of poetry in Genesis.

In Exodus, there is Moses' Song, ch. 15, with Miriam's response:

> "Sing to the Lord, for he has completely triumphed;
> The horse and its rider he has hurled into the sea."

The poetry preserved in The Book of Numbers is of especial richness and interest. It includes the beautiful blessing of Aaron, perhaps the finest of benedictions, Num. 6:24–26. This was how the priests were to bless the people forever-more:

> "The Lord bless you, and keep you!
> The Lord make his face to shine upon you, and be gracious unto you!
> The Lord lift up his countenance upon you, and give you peace!"

Two other fragments of poetry of evident antiquity appear in Num., ch. 21—the Song of the Well, vs. 17 and 18:

> "Spring up, O well! Sing to it;
> The well which the princes dug,
> Which the nobles of the people sunk,
> With the scepter, with their staffs,"

and an old satirical triumph song over the defeated Amorites, quoted from some forgotten bard of the times of the conquest, ch. 21:27–30. Finally, there are the four oracles of the Ammonite prophet Balaam, which fill chs. 23 and 24 of Numbers with blessings upon Israel, instead of the effective curses he had been brought all the way to Moab to pronounce:

> "For there can be no enchantment against Jacob,
> And no divination against Israel."

Except for a couplet in ch. 10:3 there is no poetry in Leviticus, but Deuteronomy virtually closes with another Song of Moses, ch. 32, and his blessing upon the tribes of Israel, ch. 33. It will be seen that they had a way of casting blessings and cursings in poetic form, a trait that colors the blessings and the woes in the Gospels long after, Matt. 5:1–12; Luke 6:20–26.

There is only one bit of poetry in Joshua, but it is one of the most famous and dramatic in all the Bible. Joshua, victorious over the Amorites and seeing a great victory in his very hands, cried out:

> "O sun, stop at Gibeon,
> And thou moon, at the valley of Aijalon!" (Josh. 10:12.)

The historian caught up the poet's feeling and adopted his figure, declaring that the sun stood still for a whole day, his way of saying that Joshua's victory was complete.

One of the oldest and finest of these scattered poems in the Old Testament is the War-Song of Deborah, in the fifth chapter of Judges. It goes back to 1150–1100 B.C., and its twelve scenes, rich in imagination and atmosphere, reveal the conditions of the times with amazing vividness. The poet calls the roll of the tribes concerned, contrasting the stay-at-homes with those who "exposed themselves to death, on the heights of the field." It was Deborah the prophetess who directed the campaign and sang of its success.

The poem describes the disordered state of the countryside:

> "In the time of Shamgar, the son of Anath,
> In the time of Jael, caravans had disappeared,
> And travelers kept to the by-roads;
> The peasantry had disappeared, they had disappeared in Israel,
> Until you arose, O Deborah, arose as a mother in Israel.
>
> "Armorers had they none;
> Armed men failed from the city.
> Was shield to be seen or lance,
> Among forty thousand in Israel?"

But bards at wayside springs will long recite the story of that battle to travelers, mounted or on foot:

> "O riders on tawny asses, sitting on robes;
> And you who travel on the road, attend!
> To the noise of musicians at the watering-places,
> There the triumphs of the Lord will be recounted,
> The triumphs of his peasantry in Israel."

Reuben, Dan, and Asher had not joined in the popular uprising Deborah and Barak had led, but Ephraim, Benjamin, Zebulon, Issachar, and Naphtali had rallied to their support, and won a great victory. The miserable fate of the Amorite general, slain by a woman's hand, is ironically contrasted with the great expectations of his tribe that he would return victorious and laden with spoils.

Hannah's song in I Sam., ch. 2; Samuel's denunciation of Saul, I Sam. 15:22, 23; David's reply to Goliath's challenge, I Sam. 17:45–47; his dirges over Saul and Jonathan, II Sam. 1:19–27; and over Abner, 3:33, 34; his song of victory and his farewell, II Sam. 22:1 to 23:7—these scattered pieces brighten many a page of the books of Samuel. Then there is David's inquiry of the Lord, in I Sam. 30:8, when the Amalekites had raided his village and carried off his family:

> "Shall I pursue this band?
> Shall I overtake them?"

and the divine reply:

> "Pursue, for you shall assuredly overtake,
> And as certainly, rescue."

There are fewer poetical passages in the books of Kings; Solomon's quotation from the mysterious lost book of Jashar, I Kings 8:12, and Isaiah's derisive message sent to King Hezekiah for Sennacherib, whose armies were threatening Jerusalem, II Kings 19:20–28. In I Chronicles the song David taught Asaph and his kinsmen, ch. 16, begins like Ps. 105 (vs. 1–15), though it contains lines from several others. In II Chronicles, Asa's cry to God as he went into battle against the Ethiopians, 14:11, is the only bit of poetry.

It is clear that the Hebrew historians liked to embellish their records with pieces of the early poetry of their people, and to this practice we owe a whole series of reliques of early Hebrew bards. This way of enlivening prose narratives was echoed in a lesser degree in the Apocrypha; Tobit wrote a Prayer of Rejoicing, Tobit, ch. 13, and Judith uttered a Song of Thanksgiving, Judith, ch. 16, while I Maccabees weaves into its narrative scattered stanzas from a lament over the Maccabæan persecution, in I Maccabees, 1:37–40, 2:8–13, and 3:45.

In the New Testament only one writer shows any disposition to do this, and he was a Greek, Luke, the first Christian historian. He has enriched the opening scenes of his first volume with a series of hymns composed in very much the old Jewish style, but colored with the new Christian faith. We know them by their Latin names, the Magnificat, Luke 1:46–55, the Benedictus, 1:68–79, the Gloria in Excelsis, 2:14, and the Nunc Dimittis, 2:29–32. To these should be added the Song of Elizabeth, 1:42–45. They constitute an indispensable link in the development of Jewish-Christian hymnology, which has formed an almost continuous movement over well-nigh three thousand years. But this is a development to be pursued in more detail, in connection with the great Hebrew hymn and prayer book that we call The Psalms.

CHAPTER NINE

The Poetry of the Prophets

I. THE EIGHTH CENTURY B.C.

> "We, who were prophets and priest-men
> For the kings of the east and the east-men,
> The bugles of God to the beast-men,
>   His terrible seal on our brow,—
> Physicians of music, and makers
> Of language and law, and the breakers
> Of battle, strength-lifters, heart-shakers!—
>   We are nice poets now!"[1]

S o A modern American poet has described the towering figures of the old poet-prophets of Israel. And never was poetry put to grander uses than those to which they put it! Great literatures have a way of beginning with poetry, and Hebrew literature was no exception. The oldest books in the Bible are poetry—Amos, Hosea, Micah, Isaiah—the work of the prophets of the eighth century before Christ.

AMOS

The earliest was Amos, the Judean peasant, who vigorously disclaimed the rôle and title of prophet but valiantly

---

[1] Joseph Auslander, "Word Makers," in *No Traveller Returns*.

accepted the prophet's task of standing up for the poor man
against his oppressors. He was, he protested, no prophet nor
one of the sons of the prophets, but he had heard the voice of
God calling him to speak:

> "When the lion roars,
>   who does not fear?
> When the Lord God speaks,
>   who will not prophesy?" (Amos 3:8.)

Modern social reformers usually take their texts from
Amos, for it was social injustice, the oppression of the poor by
the heartless rich, that drove him to denounce such practices
and declare that the judgment of God would inevitably overtake such oppressors, and any nation that countenanced such
selfish cruelty.

> "Because they have sold the innocent for silver,
> And the needy in exchange for a pair of sandals;
> They who trample upon the heads of the poor,
> And thrust aside the humble from the way." (Amos 2:6.)

Amos was a shepherd from south of Jerusalem, who sometimes visited the centers of the Northern Kingdom to sell his
produce, and once at Bethel, one of the principal sanctuaries
of the Northern Kingdom, he was so incensed at what he saw
and condemned it so unsparingly that the high priest ordered
him back to his own country. (Amos 7:10–17.)

> "Hear this word, you cows of Bashan,
> You who are on the mount of Samaria,
> Who oppress the weak, who crush the needy." (Amos 4:1.)

> "Therefore because you trample upon the weak,
> And take from him exactions of grain,
> Though you have built houses of hewn stone,
> You shall not dwell in them;

Though you have planted pleasant vineyards,
You shall not drink their wine. . . .
You who oppress the innocent, take bribes,
And thrust aside the needy at the gate." (Amos 5:11, 12.)

The Kingdom of Israel was flourishing under Jeroboam II, but for all its wealth and splendor Amos foresaw that a country that permitted such injustice and suffering could not escape the just judgment of God. So he became supremely the prophet of the impartial justice of God. Any nation that fattened on wickedness would perish. For Amos believed that God was not the God of the Hebrews only but held all the nations under his righteous sway.

"Take away from me the noise of your songs,
And to the melody of your lyres I will not listen.
But let justice roll down like waters,
And righteousness like a perennial stream." (Amos 5:23, 24.)

"Hear this, you who trample upon the needy,
And would bring the poor of the land to an end,
Saying, 'When will the new moon pass
That we may sell grain,
And the Sabbath that we may offer wheat for sale,'
Making the ephah small and the price great,
And falsifying the scales;
Buying the poor for silver,
And the needy in exchange for a pair of sandals,
And selling the refuse of the grain." (Amos 8:4–6.)

If you want to hear a ringing call for social and economic justice, read the little book of Amos, only eight pages long, and see what one poet-prophet of ancient Judah thought and felt about it, and had the genius to write about it, twenty-

seven hundred years ago. Amos uttered his poetic oracles between 765 and 750 B.C., and if you would read the books of
the Bible in the order in which they were written, you should
begin with Amos. He proclaimed the approach of "the day
of the Lord," which would prove a fearful Day of Judgment
not only for the surrounding nations but for Israel and
Judah too.

HOSEA

Amos was almost immediately followed by Hosea, a
prophet of the Northern Kingdom, whose work fell between
745 and 735 B.C. He was the prophet of the love of God, as
Amos had been the prophet of his justice. Hosea made his
own marriage the symbol of his teaching; his unfaithful wife
became to him the symbol of Israel's unfaithfulness to God,
while his own determination to win her back showed him how
God must long to save and restore his people. Although
Hosea foresaw national overthrow and exile as the doom of
his people, he looked beyond them to a brighter future, when
God should reclaim his people:

> "I will betroth you to myself forever;
> I will betroth you to myself in righteousness and justice,
> And in kindness and mercy." (Hosea 2:19.)

If you ever experience a great personal wrong, think of
Hosea, who found in just such a situation a revelation of the
unfailing love of God and a glimpse of how the bitterest
trials of the human heart might be sustained and redeemed
through it.

Hosea belonged not to Judah like the other poet-prophets but to the Northern Kingdom of Israel. But that did not blind him to its sins and dangers. This capacity for national self-criticism was one of the most striking traits of the Hebrew prophets.

Hosea not only rebuked his people for its deification of the forces of nature and worship of them, but for its sheer wickedness:

> "Cursing, lying, murder, theft, and adultery—
> They break out, and one crime follows hard upon another."
>
> (Hosea 4:2.)

The astounding thing about these first poet-prophets is their bold assertion that in the sight of God sacrifice and ritual matter not at all, compared with goodness, justice, and kindness to one's fellow men:

> "For it is love I delight in, and not sacrifice;
> knowledge of God, and not burnt offerings." (Hosea 6:6.)

This is why Amos and Hosea have been called the discoverers of ethical religion for mankind. They stand foremost among the great religious thinkers, the great moral pioneers of history.

The catastrophe that Amos and Hosea so clearly foresaw overtook Israel only a few years after Hosea's preaching, for in 721 B.C. Assyria, then at the height of its power, put an end to the Northern Kingdom.

The misery of the poor and humble in Judah as well as in Israel was so great that it roused another champion for them, during the days of the Prophet Hosea. His name was Micah.

MICAH

Like Amos, Micah was a peasant. He lived in a little town on the western border of Judah. Hardly three pages of his poetry have survived (Micah, chs. 1 to 3), but they are enough to set his name high among the prophets. He saw the peasantry crushed under the cruel selfishness of the rich and privileged. The cities seemed to him so full of wickedness and oppression that they became the symbols of it:

> "What is Jacob's transgression?
> Is it not Samaria?
> And what is Judah's sin?
> Is it not Jerusalem?" (Micah 1:5.)

Judges, priests, and prophets have become utterly mercenary. They care for nothing but personal gain. They are the real enemies of the nation, and they are bringing it to ruin.

The Judeans were not blind to the danger of the Northern Kingdom, but there was a widespread belief among them then and for a century after that Jerusalem would never fall; the presence of the Temple of God in it, they reasoned, would always protect it from destruction:

> "They lean upon the Lord, saying,
> Is not the Lord in the midst of us?
> No misfortune can befall us." (Micah 3:11.)

But Micah boldly declared that such sins as he saw about him, especially in Jerusalem itself, would inevitably bring ruin upon Jerusalem and even upon the Temple:

"Therefore, because of you,
   Zion shall be plowed like a field,
   And Jerusalem shall become a ruin,
   And the temple hill a high place in a forest." (Micah 3:12.)

So Micah was the first to predict that Jerusalem would be destroyed.

The little group of dirges that make up the first three chapters of Micah we may confidently date between 730 and 721 B.C., that is, between the poetry of Hosea and the fall of Samaria before the Assyrians under Sargon. To them were gradually added kindred poems by later hands, some written in the days of the Exile, and some later still. The magnificent picture of the great destiny of the Hebrews, and the golden age of peace, ch. 4:1–5, most of which appears also in Isa. 2:1–4, can never be forgotten:

"They shall beat their swords into plowshares,
   And their spears into pruning-hooks.
   Nation shall not lift up sword against nation,
   Nor shall they learn war any more.

"And they shall sit each under his vine,
   And under his fig tree, with none to frighten them;
   For the mouth of the Lord of hosts has spoken." (Micah 4:3, 4.)

Here is found the prophecy of the Messianic prince from Bethlehem:

"And you, O Bethlehem Ephrathah,
   Too little to be among the clans of Judah,
   From you, one shall come forth for me,
   Who shall be ruler over Israel,

Whose origins are from of old,
From ancient days." (Micah 5:2.)

And here is found that wonderfully simple description
of true religion which is one of the gems of religious expression:

"Yet what does the Lord require of you,
But to do justice, and to love kindness,
And to walk humbly with your God?" (Micah 6:8.)

It is not sacrifices but uprightness of life and that alone
which God demands and approves.

ISAIAH

The fourth in this great series of eighth century poet-
prophets, and the greatest of the four, was Isaiah, the prince
of prophets. He was no rustic or provincial, but a resident of
Jerusalem and a friend and counselor of the king. His work
covers forty years, for he began it in 740 B.C. and continued
it until 701. So he began before Micah and went on for
twenty years after him.

From the hour of his call to be a prophet, so grandly
described in ch. 6, Isaiah was possessed with a sense of the
holiness of God:

"Holy, holy, holy, is the Lord of hosts;
The whole earth is full of his glory." (Isa. 6:3.)

This was the song Isaiah heard the seraphs sing about the
throne of God, and it still echoes around the world at Christmas in the splendid music of the *Tersanctus*. Isaiah was

peculiarly the prophet of the holiness of God, as Amos was
of his justice, and Hosea of his love, and this sense of God's
holiness was basic in Isaiah's work.

Like Amos, Hosea, and Micah, Isaiah was keenly alive to
the wickedness about him:

> "Ah! sinful nation, guilt-laden people;
> Brood of evildoers, children who deal corruptly;
> Who have forsaken the Lord, and spurned the Holy One of
> Israel." (Isa. 1:4.)

Like them, too, he takes no stock in sacrifices offered by
guilty hands:

> " 'Of what use is the multitude of your sacrifices to me,'
> says the Lord. . . .
> 'Your hands are full of bloodshed—
> wash yourselves clean; . . .
> Cease to do evil,
> learn to do good;
> Seek justice,
> restrain the oppressor;
> Uphold the rights of the orphan,
> defend the cause of the widow!' " (Isa. 1:11, 15-17.)

Isaiah witnessed the rising power of Assyria, its conquest
of Israel in 721 B.C., and finally its attack upon Judah itself,
in 701. He sought repeatedly to mold events by advising the
king. Yet he saw in the Assyrians, ruthless and cruel as they
were, the instrument of God's vengeance:

> "O Assyria, rod of my anger,
> And staff of my fury!
> Against a godless nation I send him,

And against the people of my wrath I charge him,
To despoil them, and to prey on them,
And to trample them down like mire of the streets." (Isa. 10:5, 6.)

One of the most striking things in Isaiah is his description of the efficiency of the Assyrian army:

"None weary, none stumbling in his ranks;
He will neither slumber nor sleep.
No loin-girdle of his is loosed,
No sandal-thong is snapped;
His arrows are sharpened,
His bows are all bent;
His horses' hoofs are counted like flint,
His wheels like the whirlwind." (Isa. 5:27, 28.)

The Assyrians were indeed the scourge and terror of that ancient world.

Isaiah felt keenly his failure to stir his people to repentance and reformation, although he had expected nothing else from the moment of his call as a prophet, as related in ch. 6:

"Go and say to this people:
'Keep on hearing, but understand not;
And keep on seeing, but know not!'
Make the mind of this people gross,
Dull their ears, and besmear their eyes;
Lest they see with their eyes, and hear with their ears,
And have a mind to understand, and turn, and be healed."
(Isa. 6:9, 10.)

These words were quoted by Jesus when his message failed to move his people, Matt. 13:14, 15. Isaiah felt that a remnant at least of his people could be reached and influenced, and so resolved to bind up his testimony and seal his teaching in the hearts of his disciples, Isa. 8:16. This idea of a band of disciples within the nation, which should preserve and carry on the truth, was the germ of Judaism and of Christianity. Jesus too formed such a circle of close disciples whom he taught and trained, Mark 3:13–19.

The work of Isaiah himself may be found in chs. 1 to 39, though somewhat interspersed with the work of others, after ch. 12. The splendor of Isaiah's rhetoric led later hands to append to his book other splendid pieces of prophetic poetry, until it became a veritable anthology of the most glorious poems in Hebrew literature. Chapters 40 to 55 belong to the days of the Exile, especially toward its close when Babylon, which had conquered Judah and carried its people off into captivity, was itself facing destruction at the hands of Cyrus, the Persian conqueror (538 B.C.), Isa. 44:28; 45:1. The prospect of being free again and permitted to return to their beloved land filled the exiles with rapture, chs. 52; 55. Glorious pictures of the future splendor of Jerusalem rose before their minds, ch. 54. With ch. 56 the scene again changes, and the rest of the book, chs. 56 to 66, reflects the situations and attitudes of the following century, the fifth, as the times of Nehemiah and Ezra were approaching.

New light will fall upon the pages of Isaiah if you first read chs. 1 to 12 (excepting 9:1–17 and 11:1–9), as from the days of Isaiah, denouncing the sins of Judah and dealing with the crises brought upon Judah by the war between Israel and Syria (735, 734 B.C.) and the invasion of Sennacherib (701 B.C.). Then read chs. 13 to 23, for the most part later oracles on foreign nations, although some of them are by Isaiah. Then read chs. 28 to 31, much of which is by Isaiah. Then pass to chs. 36 to 39, which consist principally of extracts from

II Kings (chs. 18:13 to 20:19) about Sennacherib's invasion, and Isaiah's dealings with King Hezekiah.

Then read chs. 40 to 55, which picture the happiness of the exiles in Babylon a century and a half later, at the overthrow of their Babylonian oppressors:

> "Come down, and sit in the dust,
>   O virgin daughter of Babylon" (Isa. 47:1),

and their exultation at the prospect of being set free:

> "Comfort, O comfort my people,"
>   says your God;
> "Speak to the heart of Jerusalem,
>   and call to her,
> That her time of service is ended,
>   that her guilt is paid in full,
> That she has received of the Lord's hand
>   double for all her sins." (Isa. 40:1, 2.)

Then read chs. 56 to 66, with their pictures of the difficult situations in which the returned exiles found themselves, and their hopes of the golden future that still awaited God's people. For example, a passage such as the following expresses the hope for the future:

> "Arise, shine! for your light has come,
> And the glory of the Lord has risen upon you.
> For lo! darkness shall cover the earth,
> And thick darkness the peoples;
> But upon you the Lord shall rise,
> And upon you his glory shall appear;
> And nations shall walk by your light,
> And kings by the brightness of your rising." (Isa. 60:1–3.)

Finally, read chs. 24 to 27, and 32 to 35, which probably took their present form in the fourth century, after the appearance of Alexander the Great (333 B.C.).

The Book of Isaiah, therefore, is far more than one great prophet's reaction to the generation between 740 and 701 B.C.; it is a great obbligato for the whole sweep of Hebrew religious history, from Isaiah's time, through the Exile, the return, the rebuilt Temple, and the new community, and covers at least in part the Assyrian, Babylonian, Persian, and Greek periods of Jewish history.

As for the Hebrew poets of the eighth century before Christ, with their disregard of ritual and sacrifice and their clear sense of the moral demands of religion, they opened a new chapter in man's religious and moral history. And when have poets ever played so great a rôle in molding the best thought of mankind?

CHAPTER TEN

The Poetry of the Prophets

II. THE SEVENTH CENTURY B.C.

THE SPIRITUAL obbligato to the march of oriental history that the Hebrew prophets supplied was never more vivid and varied than in the single generation that witnessed the Scythian invasion, the rise of Babylon, the fall of Nineveh, and the destruction of Jerusalem, four shattering events crowded into the space of forty years.

ZEPHANIAH

The cruel suppression of the prophets under Manasseh and Amon, kings of Judah between 692 and 638 B.C., has left that period a barren one for the poetry of the prophets. Indeed, it was not until 627 B.C. that another poet-prophet made his voice heard in Judah. His name was Zephaniah, and the way in which his ancestry is pushed back to Hezekiah (Zeph. 1:1) leads us to think this must mean King Hezekiah, and that the prophet was of royal blood.

It was the appearance of the invading Scythian hordes in the north that stirred Zephaniah to speak. Herodotus speaks of them in the first book of his history, and their approach awoke the spirit of prophecy in a young contemporary of Zephaniah's, named Jeremiah (Jer. 1:13). Zephaniah saw in their approach nothing less than the dawn of the awful "day of the Lord" prophesied by Amos 150 years before.

The whole earth was to be involved in this great catastrophe, and half-heathen Judah, with all its wretched vices, was not to be spared:

> "And I will stretch out my hand against Judah,
> And against all the inhabitants of Jerusalem." (Zeph. 1:4.)

The doom which Amos had seen afar was now at hand:

> "Silence before the Lord God,
> For the day of the Lord is near at hand! . . .
> "Near at hand is the great day of the Lord;
> Near and speeding fast!
> Near at hand is the bitter day of the Lord,
> On which the warrior will cry in terror!
> A day of wrath is that day;
> A day of trouble and distress,
> A day of desolation and waste,
> A day of darkness and gloom,
> A day of cloud and thundercloud;
> A day of the trumpet and battle-cry,
> Against the fortified cities,
> And against the lofty battlements." (Zeph. 1:7, 14–16.)

It was from this prophecy (1:15) that the great medieval hymn *Dies Irae, Dies Illa,* took its text, which means "A Day of wrath is that day."

Herodotus speaks of the damage done by the Scythians
to the Philistine cities, and Zephaniah pictures it with great
vividness:

> "Gaza shall be deserted,
>   And Askelon a waste.
> Ashdod—at noon they shall expel her,
>   And Ekron shall be uprooted. . . .
> The word of the Lord is against you,
>   O Canaan, land of the Philistines!
> And I will destroy you so that there shall be no inhabitant."
>
> (Zeph. 2:4, 5.)

These nomad hordes, so like the Mongols two thousand
years later, threatened even Assyria and Egypt:

> "You, too, O Ethiopians,
>   shall be slain by my sword!
> And he will stretch out his hand against the north,
>   and destroy Assyria.
> And he will make Nineveh a desolation,
>   a drought like the desert;
> And herds shall lie down in the midst of her,
>   every beast of the field.
> Both jackdaw and hedgehog
>   shall lodge in her capitals;
> The owl shall hoot in the window,
>   the bustard on the threshold;
>   for I will destroy her city." (Zeph. 2:12–14.)

Nineveh did indeed fall only fifteen years later (612
B.C.), but it was not the Scythians but the Babylonians and
Medes that destroyed it. Two centuries later, when Xenophon
passed that way, all he could find was a great wall lying
deserted, and the very name of the city had been forgotten.
(*Anabasis*, 3:4:10.)

Like the eighth-century prophets who had gone before him, Zephaniah draws a dark picture of the depravity of Judah's leaders of all kinds. Princes, judges, priests, and prophets fall under his stern condemnation:

> "Her judges are wolves of the night,
>   Who long not for the morning.
>   Her prophets are reckless, treacherous men;
>   Her priests profane holy things;
>   They do violence to the law." (Zeph. 3:3, 4.)

You may think of Zephaniah as the prophet of the Scythian invasion of 627 B.C., which passed Judah by, for the invaders were headed for Egypt, and moved down the seacoast toward it, but Psammetichus (Psamtik I), the Pharaoh of Egypt, managed to come to terms with them and turn them back the way they had come.

NAHUM

As Zephaniah focused his attention on the threat of the Scythian invasion of 627 B.C., his brilliant contemporary Nahum dwelt upon the fall of Nineveh (612 B.C.). Assyria had been for centuries the cruel tyrant of the lands around Palestine, and her fall before the Babylonians and Medes was hailed with the greatest exultation. With extraordinary vividness Nahum describes the capture and destruction of the city:

> "Woe to the city, bloody throughout,
>   Full of lies and booty!
>   Prey ceases not.
>   The crack of the whip, and the noise of the rumbling wheel,
>   And the galloping horse, and the jolting chariot;

The charging horseman, and the flashing sword,
And the glittering spear, and a multitude of slain,
And a mass of bodies, and no end to the corpses!
They stumble over the corpses!" (Nahum 3:1–3.)

Nahum derisively calls upon the Ninevites to rally to the defense of their doomed city:

"The shatterer has come up against you;
Keep the rampart;
Watch the road; brace your loins;
Strengthen your forces to the utmost. . . .
They will make ready the chariot on that day,
And the chargers will prance.
The chariots will rage in the streets,
Dashing to and fro in the open spaces. . . .
He summons his nobles; they stumble as they go.
They hasten to the wall,
And the battering ram is set up." (Nahum 2:1–5.)

The sack of the city, then the mistress of the world, is gloatingly described:

"The gates of the rivers are opened,
And the palace melts away.
Its mistress is brought forth; she goes into captivity,
While her maidens mourn,
Moaning like the sound of doves,
Beating upon their breasts.
And Nineveh is like a pool of water,
Whose water escapes.
'Halt, halt!' they cry,
But no one turns back.
'Plunder silver, plunder gold;
For there is no end to the stores,
An abundance of all sorts of valuable articles.' " (Nahum 2:6–9.)

Judged by its own inscriptions, Assyria was the proudest and harshest of the ancient empires. What a change the prophet sees!

> "There is emptiness, desolation, and waste,
> And a melting heart and trembling knees;
> And anguish is in all loins,
> And the faces of all of them become livid.
> Where is the den of the lions,
> And the cave of the young lions,
> Whither the lion went, bringing in prey,
> The lion's cub, with none to disturb?
> Where the lion tore enough prey for his cubs,
> And rended for his lionesses,
> Filling his den with prey,
> And his lair with booty?" (Nahum 2:10–12.)

Nowhere does Hebrew poetry reach a greater height of dramatic power than in the two pages of Nahum's triumph song over Nineveh. Every line of it is eloquent, clear, and forceful. The acrostic poem (1:1–10) which introduces it probably belongs to the time of the Exile (597–538 B.C.), when such alphabetic poetry was much cultivated.

HABAKKUK

The third of the poet-prophets of the seventh century was Habakkuk. Assyria had indeed fallen, and that had brought joy to Jewish hearts, for Assyria had long been the brutal tyrant of their world. But now it began to appear that the Babylonian had simply taken the Assyrian's place, and the Hebrews had exchanged one tyrant for another. Was this to go on forever? Was this succession of cruel masters never to end? And what did it mean?

This was the question that faced Habakkuk. He grappled with it a few years after the fall of Nineveh, in the last years of the Kingdom of Judah, when Jehoiakim was king, 607–597 B.C.

Habakkuk knew that Judah was wicked and deserved to be punished:

> "How long, O Lord, must I cry for help,
>   and thou not hear?
> Call out to thee 'Violence,'
>   and thou not save?" (Hab. 1:1.)

At length an answer comes to him. God is raising up a new power to be the instrument of punishment. On the eastern horizon the Babylonians are beginning to appear!

> "Look out upon the nations and see,
>   And be utterly amazed!
>   For a deed is being done in your days
>   That you would not believe, were it told you.
>   For behold, I am raising up the Chaldeans,
>   That savage and impetuous nation,
>   That marches through the breadth of the earth,
>   To seize habitations that are not his own.
>
> "Terrible and dreadful is he;
>   Judgment and destruction go forth from him.
>   Swifter than leopards are his horses,
>   And keener than wolves of the desert.
>   His horses prance,
>   And his horsemen come from afar;
>   They swoop down like a vulture hastening to devour.
>
> "Wholly for violence does he come;
>   Terror marches before him;
>   And he gathers up captives like sand.

He makes scorn of kings,
And rulers are a joke to him!
He laughs at all fortresses,
And heaps up dirt and captures them." (Hab. 1:5–10.)

Nothing could have been more amazing to the world of the seventh century before Christ than the fall of Assyria, which had for centuries dominated the east. But the new master that has so suddenly displaced it in the control of all that region is no better than Assyria had been. Habakkuk is perplexed. He recognizes that God has established the new conqueror for chastisement, to be his instrument of punishment, but what of Babylon? Was it innocent? Why did God keep silent when the wicked swallowed up him that was more righteous than himself? (Hab. 1:13.)

"Shall he keep on emptying his net forever,
And never cease slaying the nations?" (Hab. 1:17.)

So the prophet took his stand upon his watchtower to await God's reply:

"I will take my stand upon my watchtower,
And station myself upon the rampart;
And watch to see what he will say to me,
And what answer he will make to my complaint.
Then the Lord answered me, saying,
'Write the vision clearly upon the tablets,
That one may read it on the run. . . .
Verily, the wicked man—I take no pleasure in him;
But the righteous lives by reason of his faithfulness.' "

(Hab. 2:1–4.)

It was the old problem of evil; Habakkuk does not solve it, but he knows there is nothing to be done but to keep on living the life of trust and obedience, and his statement of it became, long after, the watchword of Paul and then of Luther.

The greedy conqueror will have to pay for his crimes:

> "Because you have despoiled many nations,
>   All the rest of the peoples shall despoil you." (Hab. 2:8.)

The five woes pronounced against him, 2:6–20, denounce his rapacity, violence, and idolatry. The time is evidently that of the Babylonian invasion and conquest of Judah, and the capture of Jerusalem, 597 B.C., which began the Exile.

Habakkuk had hoped, as we do, that turning a corner in history would bring in the long-sought era of peace. It had turned out differently. After all, it must be the will of God.

> "Are not these things from the Lord of hosts,
>   That peoples exhaust themselves for the fire,
>   And nations wear themselves out for nought?
>   But the earth shall be filled with the knowledge of the glory of the Lord,
>   As the waters cover the sea." (Hab. 2:13, 14.)

The third chapter of Habakkuk is a psalm, from a much later day; it is full of echoes of Hebrew poetry, Ps. 77: 17–20, for example. But it enforces the unfailing trust in God which was Habakkuk's great conviction:

> "Though the fig tree do not flourish,
>   And there be no fruit on the vines;
>   Though the product of the olive fail,
>   And the fields yield no food;

> Though the flock be cut off from the fold,
> And there be no cattle in the stalls;
> Yet will I exult in the Lord;
> I will rejoice in my victorious God!" (Hab. 3:17, 18.)

Read Habakkuk for his indomitable faith in God in spite of the apparent triumph of injustice, oppression, and wrong.

JEREMIAH

The fourth and last of the poet-prophets of the seventh century B.C. was Jeremiah. His work, like that of Zephaniah, began with the Scythian invasion of 627 B.C., but it lasted until after the destruction of Jerusalem in 586 B.C., or more than forty years. Jeremiah lived through the tragedy of Judah—capture, destruction, exile—for, although Jeremiah did not himself go into exile in Babylonia, he witnessed that disaster. His discovery that religion was a personal rather than a corporate experience, so that it could survive the destruction of Temple and nation and still continue, we have already noted in Chapter Three, where the prose preaching of Jeremiah is mentioned.

But even Jeremiah was most eloquent in poetry. The story of his call to be a prophet, ch. 1, the dreadful prospect of invasion (4:5–31; 6:1–5, 22–26), the despair of the people (8:14–17), and the grief of the prophet (8:18 to 9:2)—these are among the most moving passages in all literature:

> "My pain is incurable,
> My heart is sick within me.
> Hark! the cry of the daughter of my people
> Far and wide through the land. . . .

'The harvest is passed, the summer is over,
And we are not saved.' . . .

"Is there no balm in Gilead?
　　Is there no physician there? . . .
O that my head were waters,
　　and my eyes a fountain of tears,
That I might weep day and night
　　for the slain of the daughter of my people!

"O that I had in the desert
　　a traveler's inn,
That I might leave my people,
　　and be quit of them!" (Jer. 8:18 to 9:2.)

No poet ever used his poetic medium more freely or boldly than did Jeremiah. It was what he had to say that was all-important:

"O land, land, land,
　　Hear the word of the Lord!" (Jer. 22:29.)

Jeremiah's denunciation of the sins of his own people and his bold declaration that Jerusalem would fall before the Babylonians alienated most of the people of Jerusalem and endangered his life. This filled him with despair and he lamented that he had ever been born:

"Woe is me, my mother! that you bore me
　　As a man of strife and a man of contention to all the earth!
　　I have neither lent nor borrowed,
　　Yet all of them curse me. . . .
　　Have I an arm of iron,
　　Or a brow of bronze?" (Jer. 15:10–12.)

"Cursed be the day on which I was born,
　　The day on which my mother bore me—

> Let it not be blessed!
> Cursed be the man who brought the good news to my father,
> 'A son is born to you'—
> Wishing him much joy!" (Jer. 20:14, 15.)

So unpopular was Jeremiah's message that he was ar-
rested and beaten and put in the stocks overnight. (Jer.
19:14 to 20:6.) He was a very sensitive man, and these cruel-
ties and indignities made him feel that even God had deceived
him:

> "Thou hast duped me, O Lord, and I let myself be duped;
> Thou hast been too strong for me, and hast prevailed.
> I have become a laughing-stock all day long,
> Everyone mocks me." (Jer. 20:7.)

His declaration that Jerusalem would fall almost cost
him his life. It was only when someone pointed out that the
Prophet Micah had said the same thing more than a century
before that saved him. (Jer., ch. 26.)

But the narrative of Jeremiah's extraordinary personal ad-
ventures is best told in the words of his famous secretary
Baruch (ch. 36; 43:6; 45:1), who was probably the compiler
of most of our books of Jeremiah. It is embodied in Jer., chs.
1; 7; 11 to 21; 25 to 29; 32 to 44; and 51:59–64, and has
been briefly summarized in Chapter Two, "Biographies."

For the poetry of Jeremiah, read chs. 1 to 23; 30; and 31.
The middle of the book, chs. 26 to 29 and 31 to 45, is almost
entirely a prose account of Jeremiah's preaching and his experiences, which seem to have been recorded by his faithful
secretary. The oracles on the nations, chs. 46 to 51, probably
owe little to Jeremiah, being mostly the work of later hands.
In fact, 46:1 to 51:58 seems to have formed an independent

book, following 25:13, with the oracles on the nations very differently arranged. Read chs. 46 to 51, therefore, as a later supplement to Jeremiah, for of these ten oracles the first of the two on Egypt (46:3–12) is the only one that can with confidence be assigned to Jeremiah.

While Jeremiah's work continued well into the sixth century B.C., two-thirds of his active years fell in the seventh, and it is with the prophets of the seventh century that he is most naturally associated.

CHAPTER ELEVEN

The Poetry of the Prophets

III. THE SIXTH AND FIFTH CENTURIES B.C.

J OY OVER the fall of Babylon and the end of the Exile found rapturous expression in the voices of the prophets, as their great hopes for the nation's destiny revived. But days of discouragement ensued, and old nationalistic rancors survived; in fact, the last of the prophets provide a veritable kaleidoscope of Hebrew religious thought, the deepest dejection alternating with the sublimest hopes.

ISAIAH CHS. 40 TO 55

The bitter experience of Exile, hard as it was, opened new religious outlooks for the Jews, and the land from which they had been carried off took on a new beauty. The prospect of deliverance from captivity and return to Judah roused poets of the Exile to the rhapsodies that are preserved in the second part of the book of Isaiah, chs. 40 to 55.

The victory of the Persians over the Jews' Babylonian masters filled the Jewish heart with joy. God had forgiven and reclaimed his people. The poet sees the highway to be prepared through the desert over which God is now to lead them home. (Isa. 40:3.)

Cyrus, the great Persian conqueror, they knew, would let them go home:

> "Thus says the Lord to his anointed,
>   To Cyrus, whose right hand I have grasped,
>   To bring down nations before him,
>   And to ungird the loins of kings, . . .
>   He shall build my city,
>   And shall set my exiles free." (Isa. 45:1, 13.)

In this deliverance, the prophets see the token of the divine forgiveness, to be proclaimed upon the mountain tops:

> "On a high mountain get you up,
>   O heralds of good news to Zion!
> Lift up your voice with strength,
>   O heralds of good news to Jerusalem!
> Lift it up, fear not;
> Say to the cities of Judah,
>   'Behold your God!' " (Isa. 40:9.)

The faithful exiles now appear as God's servant, now to be rewarded. (Isa., chs. 42; 49; 50; 52; 53.)

> "How beautiful upon the mountains
>   are the feet of the heralds,
> Who bring good news of peace,
>   news of salvation,
> Who say to Zion,
>   'Your God has became king.' " (Isa. 52:7.)

The downfall of Babylon and its gods is exultingly described in chs. 46 and 47. This part of Isaiah ends in ch. 55 with a great song of jubilation:

"Ho! everyone that is thirsty, come to the waters,
And he that has no money, come, buy, and eat!
Come, buy grain without money,
And wine and milk without price! . . .
For with joy shall you go out,
And in peace shall you be led;
The mountains and the hills shall break into singing before you,
And all the trees of the field shall clap their hands."

(Isa. 55:1, 12.)

Some twenty years later, in 520 and 519 B.C., the Prophets Haggai and Zechariah stirred the returned exiles to rebuild the Temple, but they do not belong to the great series of the poet-prophets. Haggai preached in prose, and we have considered his work in the chapter on Hebrew oratory (Three). Zechariah was one of the first of the prophets to employ apocalyptic in his preaching (we have seen its beginnings in Ezekiel); and he will therefore be considered in the chapter on "Visions and Revelations." But their words find echoes in the poetry of the last part of Isaiah, chs. 56 to 66.

ISAIAH CHS. 56 TO 66

While the second part of Isaiah, chs. 40 to 55, clearly reflects the time of the overthrow of the Babylonian Empire by the Persians under Cyrus, 538 B.C., and Jewish anticipations of return to Palestine, the third and final part of the book, chs. 56 to 66, as we have seen, belongs to the times of the restored Jewish community in Jerusalem, in the early part of the fifth century before Christ. Greatly influenced by Isa., chs. 40 to 55, as well as by the utterances of Haggai and Zechariah (520, 519 B.C.), it invites aliens and

eunuchs to unite with the struggling little community, ch. 56,
boldly exposes the immoralities of idolatry, ch. 57, and rein-
terprets fasting, Sabbath observance, and repentance, chs. 58
and 59. Poor as the community was, the prophet still believes
in a bright and golden future, chs. 60 and 65.

MALACHI

To the same period, 475–450 B.C., belongs the prophecy
of Malachi. The return to Palestine had been a disappointment. Few of the exiles had taken advantage of the opportunity Cyrus had given them to go back to Judah. Stirred by
the preaching of Haggai and Zechariah, in 519 B.C., the
people had rebuilt the Temple, but the walls of Jerusalem
still lay in ruins. The Temple worship had been resumed, but
in so mean and half-hearted a fashion that Malachi would
rather see the Temple closed and the service discontinued,
1:10. The people are careless about their religious duties, the
priesthood is neglectful of its work, and religion is at a low
ebb.

The little book of Malachi was once a sort of appendix
to Zechariah and takes its name from the word Malachi,
which means "My Messenger," in 3:1, the most striking
oracle in the little book; it may have been the prophet's name.
He seeks to stir his sluggish, negligent people to some sense
of their religious responsibilities with threats of the approach
of a Day of Judgment:

> "You have wearied the Lord with your statements.
> Yet you say, 'How have we wearied him?' . . .
> Behold, I will send forth my messenger,
> And he shall prepare the way before me! . . .

> Who can endure the day of his coming?
> And who can stand when he appears?
> For he shall be like a refiner's fire,
> And like fullers' soap,
> And he shall sit down as a refiner and cleanser of silver,
> And shall cleanse the sons of Levi." (Mal. 2:17 to 3:3.)

The morals of the nation shall be purified, 3:5, and the people will again pay their tithes and make their offerings as they should:

> "Should man rob God?
> Yet you are robbing me!
> But you say, 'How have we robbed thee?'
> In the tithe and the contribution! . . .
> Bring the whole tithe into the storehouse,
> That there may be food in my house,
> And test me now in this way," says the Lord of hosts,
> "And see if I will not open for you the windows of the heavens,
> And pour out for you a blessing until there is no more need."
>
> (Mal. 3:8–10.)

In a magnificent passage, the prophet declares that God is in no need of them:

> "For from the rising of the sun, even to its setting,
> My name is great among the nations;
> And in every place an offering is made, is presented to my name,
> And a pure offering.
> For my name is great among the nations,"
> Says the Lord of hosts. (Mal. 1:11.)

The prophet here recognizes that God accepts heathen worship, if it is sincere, whether offered in Jewish ways or not—an extraordinary insight into religious reality.

From Mal. 3:1 the first Evangelist long after took the
lines with which he introduced John the Baptist (Mark 1:2),
and from Mal. 4:5 arose John's identification as a returning
Elijah, Matt. 11:14–17; Mark 9:11–13.

Malachi is one of the few prophets who is deeply concerned
for both moral behavior and ritual observance on the part of
the people.

OBADIAH

Palestine was and is a small country, but none the less,
perhaps all the more, prone to disturbance and dissension. It
was not only the great overshadowing powers, Egypt, Assyria,
and Babylon, that concerned the prophets, but their smaller
and nearer neighbors, Syria, Philistia, Moab, Ammon, and
Edom. Beyond Edom were the Arabs, then as now a force in
the life of those regions.

Between Judah and Edom a feud had long been smolder-
ing; even before Jeremiah, one prophet had cried out against
Edom and his words are echoed in Jer. 49:14–16, 9, 10, and
7; they also form the text of Obadiah's little two-page
prophecy, Obad. 1–7.

The Jews had a long score to settle with the Edomites, or
so they thought. They had taken advantage of the Jewish
disaster, when Jerusalem fell before the Babylonians; instead
of helping the vanquished, they had given their aid to the
victors and joined in betraying and plundering their neighbors. But Esau should have helped his brother Jacob. The
Edomites were Judah's nearest neighbors on the south, and
they had helped themselves to what they could get of Judah's

territory. The Jews in exile in Babylonia were well aware of what was going on. Ezekiel put it very plainly:

Thus says the Lord God: "In the fire of my indignation I speak against the rest of the nations, and against Edom, the whole of it, who with intense glee and maliciousness of heart took over my land as a possession for themselves, to hold it as a prey."

But now, in Obadiah's time, there are signs that Edom is going to be requited for her perfidy and rapacity. The Arabs are beginning to serve her as she had served Judah. They are crowding up from the southeast against Edom. Obadiah sees in this movement Edom's punishment for its faithless behavior when Judah was in similar straits, and the fulfilment of the prophecy quoted by Jeremiah long before:

> "We have heard a message from the Lord,
> And a messenger has been sent forth among the nations:
> 'Arise! Let us rise up against her for battle.' " (Obad. 1.)

The Edomites lived in rocky heights difficult of access but easy to protect:

> "The pride of your heart has deceived you,
> You who dwell in the clefts of the cliff,
> And set your dwelling on high,
> And say to yourself,
> 'Who can bring me down to the earth?'
> Though you build your nest high like the eagle,
> And set your nest even among the stars,
> From there I will bring you down," is the oracle of the Lord.
> (Obad. 3, 4.)

Obadiah is evidently quoting this from the ancient prophet whom Jeremiah had quoted somewhat freely, in order to point out that it is beginning to be fulfilled, and to recall the crimes against Judah that Edom had committed:

> "On the day when you stood by,
>   While aliens carried off his goods,
>   And foreigners entered his gates,
>   And cast lots upon Jerusalem,
>   You, too, were as one of them.
>
> "You should not have gloated over your brother,
>   on the day of his adversity.
>   You should not have rejoiced over the Judeans,
>   on the day of their ruin. . . .
>   As you have done, it shall be done to you;
>   Your deed shall return upon your own head." (Obad. 11, 12, 15.)

This dark strain of hatred for Edom runs through many of the prophetical books, Amos (1:11, 12), Jeremiah, Isaiah, and Joel (3:19), but it forms the sole theme of Obadiah's book, the shortest in the Old Testament.

Obadiah's little prophecy was uttered probably about 400 B.C. Almost a century later, in 312 B.C., the Arab encroachment upon the Edomites reached its climax in the capture of Petra, the rock-hewn capital and citadel of the Edomites, which is still one of the wonders left to us from antiquity. It was probably then that the final doom was pronounced upon Edom, preserved in the latest part of Isa., ch. 34:

> "You nations, draw near to listen;
>   You peoples, attend! . . .
>   For in the heavens my sword has drunk its fill;
>   And see! it descends upon Edom,
>   For judgment upon the people whom I have doomed. . . .
>   For the Lord has a day of vengeance,
>   A year of requital for the feud against Zion;

And the rivers of Edom will be turned into pitch,
And her dust into brimstone. . . .
She will become a haunt of jackals,
An inclosure for ostriches;
Desert demons will join goblins,
And satyrs will meet one another; . . .
There will the vultures gather,
None without her mate." (Isa. 34:1, 5, 8, 9, 13–15.)

JOEL

In Palestine, as in some parts of the United States, a plague of locusts was sometimes an indescribable calamity. With such an affliction, The Book of Joel begins:

"What the shearer left, the locust ate,
And what the locust left, the hopper ate,
And what the hopper left, the stripper ate. . . .
For a nation has come up against my land,
Strong and innumerable;
His teeth are a lion's teeth,
And the fangs of a lioness are his. . . .
The field is devastated;
The ground mourns." (Joel 1:4, 6, 10.)

The famine is so severe that the offerings for the Temple cannot be provided, and the Temple service is suspended. The cattle are starving. Even the wild animals are dying. (Joel 1:17–19.)

The priests and the elders led the people in a great appeal to God for aid. A fast was proclaimed, and a great meeting held. The nation repented and called upon God to deliver them, 2:12–17.

He answered their united prayer and had pity on his people. The locusts were swept into the desert and the sea.

and the winter and spring rains came, as of old. Once more there was the promise of plenty, 2:18–27.

The plague of locusts seemed to Joel to portend the coming of the terrible "day of the Lord," which the prophets had been predicting for almost three centuries, or ever since the time of Amos, 2:11. But now he has a vision of a brighter future, when the Spirit of the Lord will speak to young and old, high and low:

> "It shall come to pass afterward,
> That I will pour out my spirit upon all flesh;
> Your sons and your daughters shall prophesy;
> Your old men shall dream dreams,
> And your young men shall see visions.
> Furthermore, upon the male and female slaves,
> In those days I will pour out my spirit." (Joel 2:28, 29.)

This magnificent prospect was claimed by the early Christians as the charter for their movement, Acts 2:17ff.

Joel still, in prose and in poetry, called for God's judgment upon the heathen, 3:1–13; but beyond the storms he too sees a golden age for Judah and Jerusalem:

> "Judah shall abide forever,
> And Jerusalem throughout the ages." (Joel 3:20.)

Joel shows acquaintance with many earlier Jewish writers, and probably wrote his poems about 400 B.C. But in his four pages he said much to cheer the discouraged little community in Jerusalem, and to keep alive the unconquerable hope of his people.

CHAPTER TWELVE

Popular Religious Poetry

I T W A S a great thing that such poets as Amos, Hosea, Isaiah, and a dozen others we can name spoke for religion among the Hebrews. But it was just as great a thing when deep religious experiences found worthy expression on the lips of a multitude of minor poets whose names have been forgotten. For their words too have survived, and quickened the religious lives of millions. The literary prophets are generally regarded as the finest feature of our heritage from Israel, but no less influential have been these unknown poets among the people whose songs and prayers are often dearer to our hearts than the oracles of the prophets. For beyond most of the prophets they express personal religious experience and devotion.

THE PSALMS

Of all the books of the Bible, the book of Psalms is for a great many people the best loved, and yet at the same time it is for others the most confused and bewildering. For it passes directly from one religious mood to another, totally different, but expressed with the same intensity of feeling. It is a veritable kaleidoscope of religious experience. It is in some respects the most familiar book in the Bible, for many lovers of the Bible can still repeat many of the psalms from memory. Certainly the greatest psalms play a notable part in the religious life of great numbers of us today.

As it stands, the book of Psalms may be described as the hymn book and the prayer book of the second Temple, the one built in 520–516 B.C. by the Jewish exiles who returned to Jerusalem, aided by the Jews who had managed to remain in the land, and their descendants. But the Psalter was a gradual growth and the work of many hands. Earlier collections of psalms preceded this one and formed parts of it. It is a collection of collections, which is why it contains some duplicates, certain psalms appearing in it more than once. Thus Ps. 53 repeats Ps. 14; Ps. 70 repeats Ps. 40:14–17, and Ps. 108 consists of Ps. 57:7–11 and Ps. 60:5–12. The earliest of these collections was Ps. 1 to 41; Ps. 42 to 89 formed the second, and Ps. 90 to 150 the third. Behind and within these, smaller collections may be identified by their titles, Psalms of the Sons of Korah, 42 to 49, and those of the Sons of Asaph, 73 to 83. These were the names of guilds of Temple singers, referred to in II Chron. 20:19 and 29:30.

The Jews, who liked to ascribe their laws to Moses and their proverbs to Solomon, called the Psalter the Psalms of David, or simply David, but as a matter of fact very few psalms indeed can be assigned to the eighth century before Christ, and most of them are later than 400 B.C. Among the oldest are Ps. 24:7–10 (perhaps occasioned by the bringing of the Ark from Shiloh to the Temple in Jerusalem, II Sam., ch. 6), and Ps. 45, which has been called a royal marriage song.

The line of the Old Testament prophets ended about 400 B.C. with Obadiah and Joel, and one might feel that a decay in religion must have ensued in Judah. But now arose this wealth of personal religious expression that we find in The Psalms, and who can say that it was less significant or influential than the prophets had been? In The Psalms, Jewish religion, which had been so largely national and official, becomes personal; we may almost say democratic. Certainly it is not confined to the hands of a few priests or prophets, but now finds rich expression from scores of hearts. More than ever before, The Psalms tell us, Judaism now became a personal experience and found individual expression. This is the great religious meaning of the book of Psalms. It is a great collection of personal religious experience. It is this that has so endeared it to every Christian generation.

These expressions range all the way from the deepest, almost despairing sense of sin and guilt (130) and appeals for God's help (22; 25), to hope and trust (16), gratitude for God's goodness (21; 92), and his personal care (23), fellowship with him (73), delight in his word (119), and in the glory of nature (19), praise of him (95; 136; 148; 149), and a sense of the glory of God (96). The old prophetic concern for uprightness of life and justice in human relations appears in Ps. 12 and 15.

The Psalms themselves doubtless owed much to earlier religious models, for the Babylonians had their penitential psalms, the Ras Shamra tablets include ancient hymns, and one Egyptian hymn of Amenhotep IV, 1370 B.C., is clearly reflected in Ps. 104. But the great experiences of the Jewish people—exile, persecution, deliverance, worship—are all reflected here. The Psalter is not free from hymns of hate (the so-called imprecatory psalms), but these are remarkably few, Ps. 69; 109; 137, and are obviously national rather than personal. They reflect the long-cherished bitter memories of subjugation, deportation, and exile in Babylon, handed down from generation to generation. Some preserve bitter memories of the old feud with Edom:

> "Remember, O Lord, against the Edomites,
> The day of Jerusalem!" (Ps. 137:7.)

Some psalms delight in the revelation of God in nature. The Nineteenth finds him glorified in the material and the moral universe:

> "The heavens are telling the glory of God,
> And the sky shows forth the work of his hands.
> Day unto day pours forth speech,
> And night unto night declares knowledge." (Ps. 19:1, 2.)

Some of the psalms are historical, tracing the hand of God in Hebrew history, Ps. 78; 105; 106; 107; 136.

We might call The Psalms the poetry of the priests, not because it was all written by priests, though much of it no doubt came from them or their brethren the Temple Levites, but because they made it theirs through preserving and arranging it, and using it in the prayers and hymns of the Temple service.

The ancient uses of these hymns and prayers were varied. Some were sung by pilgrims as they went up to the Temple for the Passover:

> "I was glad when they said to me,
> 'Let us go to the house of the Lord.' " (Ps. 122:1.)

Some reveal the satisfaction of the pilgrims as they beheld the walls and towers of their Holy City:

> "Encircle Zion and walk around her;
>   Count her towers;
>   Set your mind upon her wall;
>   Go through her palaces." (Ps. 48:12, 13.)

Others take the reader into the Temple, to enjoy its solemnities:

> "Come into his gates with thanksgiving,
>   And into his courts with praise!" (Ps. 100:4.)

Many of the psalms must have been used in the Temple service; they are liturgy and were written for that purpose, like the great antiphony of Ps. 136, where the leader uttered the line, and the chorus of Levites or the whole congregation made the response:

> "Give thanks to the Lord, for he is good,
>   For his kindness is everlasting,"

this response or refrain being given twenty-six times.
One describes a religious procession in the sanctuary:

> "Singers lead; at the rear, the stringed instruments;
>   In the middle, maidens playing timbrels.
>   In choirs, they bless God."
>   (Ps. 68:25, 26.)

Some of the instruments used in these processions are mentioned in Ps. 150, the last of a group of five Hallelujah

Psalms that conclude the book—the horn, the lyre, the lute, the drum, the strings, the pipe, and the clanging cymbals.

In the longest of the psalms, 119, the poet rejoices in the possession of the Law, his great book of religion:

> "O how I love thy law!
> It is my meditation all day long. . . .
> Thy word is a lamp to my feet,
> And a light on my path." (Ps. 119:97, 105.)

In form, a few psalms are acrostics, a form of art that appeals to the eye, not always to the ear. In its simplest form the first clause or sentence begins in Hebrew with the first letter of the Hebrew alphabet, the next with the second, and so on through the twenty-two letters. Psalms 111; 112 are of this kind. In more elaborate acrostics, a stanza of two lines may begin with each letter, as in Ps. 34, or one of four lines, as in Ps. 37, or even of eight, as in Ps. 119, where all the lines of a stanza begin with the same letter. Of course, this playful form of art baffles the translator, and he has taken refuge in the obscure device of heading each line or group of lines with the Hebrew letter, Aleph, Beth, Gimel, and so forth, with which the lines in each division begin, but this hardly conveys to the reader what is intended. Other acrostic psalms are 9; 10; 25; and 145. The same form of poetic art is found in Nahum, ch. 1, Prov., ch. 31, and Lam., chs. 1 to 4.

Although some psalms express national emotions, the most striking thing about them is their expression of personal religious experience. This is what has made them live in the religious life of every generation since they were written. The Psalter was completed in the second century before Christ, and the so-called Psalms of Solomon were produced by the Pharisees largely under their influence in the following century. Our first Christian hymns, the canticles of Luke, chs. 1 and 2, are strongly influenced by the psalms, and the second-century Christian hymns discovered in 1909 and known as the Odes of Solomon also owe much to the Psalter, as does Christian hymnology ever since.

It is when the psalmists reach out to God, not only in history and in nature, but in personal experience, that they touch us most closely. It is this that has made such a place for the book of Psalms in the affections of the modern religious world. Of all the psalms the most universally known and loved is the Twenty-third. The Ninetieth brings home to us the solemn sense of the shortness of life, and finds refuge in the mercy of God.

The heart's thirst for God is wonderfully set forth in Ps. 42:

> "As a deer longs for the water-courses,
> So my whole being longs for thee, O God."

The psalmist's confidence in God finds repeated expression:

> "God is our refuge and strength,
> A well-proved help in trouble." (Ps. 46:1.)

Even the most despairing of the psalms—the Twenty-second, which begins: "My God, my God, why hast thou forsaken me?" the words uttered by Jesus on the cross (Mark 15:34)—ends with the acknowledgment of deliverance, vs. 23–31.

Great interest attaches to the little group of psalms sung at the Passover supper, the Hallel, Ps. 113 to 118, Ps. 113 and 114 being sung before the supper and Ps. 115 to 118 after it. These last were, therefore, the hymn referred to in the Gospels: "After singing the hymn they went out of the city and up the Mount of Olives." (Mark 14:26.)

While The Psalms may be read continuously, as the three earlier collections (united in our book of Psalms about 150 B.C.), that is, first Ps. 1 to 41, then Ps. 42 to 89, and finally Ps. 90 to 150—many of them call for closer, more reflective reading as individual poems.

Every reader will find his own favorite psalms, but most selections will include Ps. 1; 8; 19; 23; 24; 42; 84; 90; 91; 98; 121; 122; 125; 126; 130. But of course this is numerically only one-tenth of the whole and is far from exhausting its chief treasures.

THE HYMNS IN THE GOSPEL OF LUKE

This strain of Hebrew psalmody passes nobly into Christian literature with the four hymns that meet us in the first chapters of the Gospel of Luke. Indeed, we should rather say five, for the words of Elizabeth as she greeted her kinswoman Mary are themselves a poem:

> "You are the most favored of women,
>   And blessed is your child!
>   Who am I,
>   To have the mother of my Lord come to me?
>
> "For the moment your greeting reached my ears,
>   The child stirred with joy within me!

Blessed is she who has believed,
For what the Lord has promised her will be fulfilled!"
(Luke 1:42–45.)

Mary's response is the Magnificat, a splendid Messianic hymn in four stanzas, rich in echoes of the Old Testament, especially The Psalms:

"My heart extols the Lord,
My spirit exults in God my Savior.
For he has noticed his slave in her humble station,
For from this time all the ages will think me favored! . . .

"He has done mighty deeds with his arm,
He has routed the proud-minded,
He has dethroned monarchs and exalted the poor,
He has satisfied the hungry with good things, and sent the rich
away empty-handed.

"He has helped his servant Israel,
Remembering his mercy,
As he promised our forefathers
To have mercy on Abraham and on his descendants forever!"
(Luke 1:46–48, 51–55.)

While the Magnificat bears much resemblance to Hannah's song, in I Sam. 2:1–10, it is clear that the birth of the expected child is to usher in the fulfilment of God's long-promised mercy to his people. Mary's song is to that extent Messianic and Christian.

The song of Zechariah, the Benedictus, in five stanzas, Luke 1:68–79, is even more strongly colored by the language of The Psalms. It rejoices over the birth of John the Baptist:

"And you, my child, will be called a prophet of the Most High,
For you will go before the Lord to make his way ready,

Bringing his people the knowledge of salvation
Through the forgiveness of their sins.

"Because the heart of our God is merciful,
And so the day will dawn upon us from on high,
To shine on men who sit in darkness and the shadow of death,
And guide our feet into the way to peace." (Luke 1:76–79.)

The child John is to become the forerunner of the mighty Savior, of the house of David.

The third of these ancient hymns is the Gloria in Excelsis, "Glory to God in the highest," that is, in heaven—the song of the heavenly host, praising God for the birth of Christ, Luke 2:14. The fourth is the utterance of the aged Symeon, as he took the infant Messiah in his arms:

"Now, Master, you will let your slave go free
In peace, as you promised,
For my eyes have seen your salvation
Which you have set before all the nations,
A light of revelation for the heathen,
And a glory to your people Israel!" (Luke 2:29–32.)

This song is familiar to many in the words of the King James Version: "Lord, now lettest thou thy servant depart in peace, according to thy word: for mine eyes have seen thy salvation, which thou hast prepared before the face of all people; a light to lighten the Gentiles, and the glory of thy people Israel."

In these earliest Christian hymns, from the first century after Christ, we see the stream of Hebrew psalmody entering Christian channels, later to expand into the vast wealth of Christian hymnology, ancient, medieval, and modern. By the middle of the second century, as we have seen, such a body of Christian hymns as the so-called Odes of Solomon was written, strongly reminiscent of the Old Testament Psalms, but full of the new religious experience that we recognize as Christian. So in The Psalms and the religious poetry that followed them, Jeremiah's great discovery of the personal character of religion more and more came into its rightful place, and scores of unknown poets among the people offered their sacrifice of praise.

CHAPTER THIRTEEN

Laments and Dirges

THE FAMILIAR experience of bereavement and loss found eloquent expression in Hebrew literature in dirges and laments. The Old Testament is full of them. The short pieces of poetry that we can with most confidence ascribe to David are of this kind, such as his lament over Saul and Jonathan, II Sam. 1:19–27:

> "Your beauty, O Israel,
> Upon your heights is slain.
> How have the heroes fallen! . . .
> How have the mighty fallen,
> And the weapons of war perished!"

When David's captain Joab murdered Saul's general Abner, David attended the funeral and chanted a dirge for Abner:

> "Should Abner die as dies the wanton fool? . . .
> As one falls before bandits, you have fallen." (II Sam. 3:33, 34.)

And there is David's lament over Absalom: "My son Absalom, my son, my son Absalom! O that I, even I, had died instead of you, Absalom, my son, my son!" (II Sam. 19:1.)

The prophets sometimes uttered dirges and laments.

116

Amos, the first of the poet-prophets, utters a similar brief dirge over Israel:

"Hear this word that I am taking up concerning you, a dirge, O house of Israel:

> "Fallen, never to rise again,
>   is the virgin Israel;
> Prostrate on her own soil,
>   with none to raise her up." (Amos 5:1, 2.)

The second poem in Micah, 1:10–16, is a dirge for Israel:

> "Tell it not in Gath!
> Weep bitterly in Bethel;
>   roll yourselves in dust!"

Jeremiah, who witnessed such lamentable events in the national life of Judah, uttered a piteous lament over the fate confronting Zion:

> "Consider and call for the mourning women, that they may come,
> And send for the skilful women, that they may make haste,
> And raise a lament over us,
> Till our eyes run down with tears,
> And our eyelids gush with water!
> For hark! a wail is heard from Zion:
> 'How we are ruined!
> We are bitterly ashamed, because we have had to leave our land,
> Because we have had to give up our dwellings.' . . .
> Teach your daughters a lamentation,
> Each one her neighbor a dirge:
> 'Death has climbed through our windows,
>   has entered our halls,
> Cutting off the children from the streets,
>   the young men from the squares.' " (Jer. 9:17–21.)

Jeremiah's lament for the king and the queen-mother,
13:18, 19, is followed by another lament for Jerusalem, 13:
20–27:

> "If you say to yourself,
>   'Why have these things befallen me?'
> It is for your many sins. . . .
> Can the Ethiopian change his skin,
>   or the leopard his spots?
> Then may you also do good,
>   who are trained to do evil." (Jer. 13:22, 23.)

Ezekiel, too, uttered lamentations over Judah's foes; over
Tyre, 27:1–36, alternating poetry with prose. He describes
maritime Tyre as a beautiful ship:

> "O Tyre, you have said,
>   'I am perfect in beauty';
> Your domain was in the heart of the seas,
>   your builders made you perfect in beauty." (Ezek. 27:3, 4.)

An extraordinary paragraph of prose, 27:12–25, tells of
the immense range of Tyre's trade, and the commodities and
luxuries in which she dealt. But at last the mariners'

> "daughters shall raise a dirge for you,
>   and lament over you:
> 'Who has been ruined like Tyre
>   in the heart of the sea?' . . .
>   for you have come to an awful end,
>   and shall be no more forever." (Ezek. 27:32, 36.)

The ancient historians say that Tyre was indeed besieged
by Nebuchadnezzar for thirteen years, in one of history's

most famous sieges, probably 585 to 573 B.C., but did not fall. Ezekiel even utters a dirge over the king of Tyre, 28:11–19:

" 'You have come to an awful end, and shall be no more forever.' "

The desolation of Egypt by Nebuchadnezzar also fell short of Ezekiel's anticipations, expressed in his dirge over Pharaoh, 32:1–16, and over Egypt, 32:17–32: Egypt is pictured as going down to Sheol, the abode of the dead, and taking her place there with the departed empires of the past, Assyria, Elam, Edom, and the rest, surrounded by the uncounted numbers of those who have fallen by the sword. But, while Nebuchadnezzar succeeded in checking Egypt, he did not conquer it or add Egypt to his empire.

Some of the psalms, too, are really in substance laments: 22; 79; 83; and perhaps also 12; 28; 80; 85; and 123. Certainly they are closely akin to Lam., ch. 5. The satirical account in Rev., ch. 18, of the lamentations of kings, merchants, dealers, and mariners over the destruction of Babylon-Rome presents a New Testament example of this type of literature.

LAMENTATIONS

The greatest examples of the Hebrew dirge are found in The Book of Lamentations, or Dirges, long connected, though for no good reason, with the name of Jeremiah. The book consists of four such dirges, dealing with the fall of Jerusalem before the Babylonians, in 597 and 586 B.C., and the consequent miseries of the king and people, followed by a prayer for God's mercy. The first four chapters are acrostic poems, like the Praise of the Good Wife, in Prov., ch. 31, and no less than nine of the psalms, 9–10; 25; 34; 37; 111; 112; 119; and 145.

Curiously enough, although the first poem in Lamentations follows the present order of the Hebrew alphabet, in the second, third, and fourth, letters fifteen and sixteen are transposed, to form what was probably an older order—as if in our alphabet *j* followed *k*. The practice of writing poems in acrostics was, as we have seen, a late development in Hebrew literature. The first, second, and third chapters are in stanzas of three lines each; the fourth is in two-line stanzas. The first stanza of each chapter begins with the first letter of the Hebrew alphabet, the second with the second, and so on through its twenty-two letters. But in the third chapter, all three lines of the first stanza begin with the first letter, all three of the second with the second, and so on, very much as in Ps. 119. Chapters 1 to 4 are all in the Hebrew elegiac meter.

Lamentations is probably the least read of the books of the Old Testament, partly because of its title, which is certainly not attractive. Yet in its realm of bitter grief and dejection, it possesses great beauty and exquisite pathos. The first dirge, written probably about 500 B.C., still broods over the misery of the sacked and ruined city:

> "How lonely the city sits,
>   once so crowded with people! . . .
> She that was a princess among the **cities**
>   has become a vassal. . . .
> Judah has been carried into exile, . . .
> She has to live among the nations,
>   she can find no home. . . .

> Her people are all moaning,
>> in their search for bread;
> They give of their treasures for food,
>> to keep themselves alive. . . .
> Ho, all you who pass along the road,
>> look and see,
> If there is any pain like my pain,
>> which has been dealt to me." (Lam. 1:1, 3, 11, 12.)

There is something terribly modern about all this dreadful Jewish catastrophe that brings the old forgotten book to life again before our very eyes. It is such memories of unforgotten grief that has led the Jews for centuries to wail aloud and kiss and caress the walls of Herod's Temple, from the ruins of which they are excluded; though a wiser course is that proposed by Jeshua in Ecclesiasticus: "Do not resign your heart to grief" was his counsel, Ecclus. 38:20.

The second dirge, Lam., ch. 2, pictures the destruction of Jerusalem in 586 B.C., and sees in it the judgment of God upon his own people. The misery of the starving children is especially felt:

> "To their mothers they keep saying,
>> 'Where is there grain and wine?' (Lam. 2.12.)
> "Lift up your hands to him
>> for the life of your children,
> Who faint for hunger
>> at the head of every street." (Lam. 2:19.)

Chapters 2 and 4 may be as old as the Exile and date from about 560 B.C.

In the third chapter, the city speaks in the first person, almost as if the speaker were the unfortunate Jehoiachin, who became king at eighteen, and after a reign of three months was a prisoner in Babylon for thirty-six years. The poet recognizes that God has punished him, and tries to adjust himself to his wretched lot:

> "It is good for a man,
>> that he should bear the yoke in his youth." (Lam. 3:27.)

He acknowledges his own sin, but closes with an earnest appeal for vengeance upon his persecutors, 3:64–66. This most elaborate of the four acrostics is the latest in date of the five poems, and was probably written in the third century before Christ.

In the fine dirge which forms the fourth chapter, the wretched condition of the pillaged city is feelingly described:

> "How dim the gold has become,
>> how changed the finest gold!
> The sacred stones are being thrown out
>> at the head of every street. . . .
> The precious children of Zion,
>> comparable to fine gold, . . .
> The children are begging bread,
>> with none to offer it to them. . . .
> Better off are those stricken by the sword
>> than those stricken by hunger; . . .
> Men dog our footsteps,
>> so that we cannot walk in our public squares."
>> (Lam. 4:1, 2, 4, 9, 18.)

All this has a sadly realistic sound today. And yet these sufferings had not softened the Hebrew heart, for the poet closes with the hope that his enemy Edom may suffer as bitterly for its crimes as Jerusalem had suffered.

The last chapter of Lamentations is a piteous statement,

on behalf of the nation, of the miseries it had suffered, with its capital desolated. Though it probably dates from the latter part of the sixth century before Christ, about 530 B.C., it might have been written yesterday:

> "Our heritage has been turned over to aliens,
> Our homes to foreigners. . . .
> Our drinking-water we have to buy;
> Our wood comes only by purchase.
> With a yoke on our necks we are persecuted;
> We toil without rest. . . .
> Slaves rule over us,
> With none to free us from their power; . . .
> Our skin glows like a fire pot,
> With the fever heat of famine.
> Women are ravished in Zion,
> Girls in the cities of Judah.
> Princes are hanged by their hands;
> Elders are not respected.
> Young men have to carry the mill,
> And youths stumble under loads of wood."
>
> (Lam. 5:2, 4, 5, 8, 10–13.)

Read The Book of Lamentations for its graphic account of the unforgettable agonies of the Hebrew people in the destruction of their capital and their people in 586 B.C.—agonies so often renewed and repeated in later Jewish experience in ancient, medieval, and modern times.

CHAPTER FOURTEEN

The Poetry of the Philosophers

SIDE BY SIDE with priests and prophets there gradually arose in later Judaism another group of thinkers and writers, the wise men, or sages—or as we would call them, the philosophers. They too expressed themselves chiefly in poetry. They did not, it is true, devise elaborate systems; their thinking was done mostly within the framework of Jewish religion, and their philosophy was built upon belief in the moral government of God. It was therefore practical rather than speculative and found its chief expression in countless maxims for the conduct of daily life, which we call proverbs. But it sometimes rose to longer poems on Wisdom, which it conceived as one of the chief attributes of God, and one which it was the chief glory of man to seek to cultivate. So, although the Jews knew nothing of science, as the Babylonians did, they yet were feeling their way toward an understanding of human relations and social intercourse.

PROVERBS

Of such wisdom they regarded Solomon as the founder and chief example. The First Book of Kings declares that he uttered three thousand proverbs, 4:32. The title of The Book of Proverbs describes it as The Proverbs of Solomon, though other authors, Agur and Lemuel, are mentioned in 30:1 and 31:1. Some of the proverbs are of Egyptian origin, for a series of thirty, of different lengths, in 22:17 to 24:22, has been shown to be translated from an Egyptian work, the Wisdom of Amen-em-ope, a sage who lived some time between 1000 and 600 B.C.

The purpose of the Hebrew sages is finely put in the opening lines of Proverbs:

> "That men may gain wisdom and instruction,
>   May understand words of intelligence;
>   That they may receive instruction in wise conduct,
>   In rectitude, justice, and honesty;
>   That sense may be imparted to the simple,
>   Knowledge and discretion to the inexperienced—
>   The wise man also may hear and increase his learning,
>   The man of intelligence acquire sound principles—
>   That they may understand proverb and parable,
>   The words of the wise and their epigrams." (Prov. 1:2–6.)

This fine educational program clearly aims at mental and moral training that will result in wise conduct. Its religious basis is immediately stated:

> "Reverence for the Lord is the beginning of knowledge."
>   (Prov. 1:7.)

The poetry of Proverbs and of the Wisdom literature in general—Ecclesiastes in the Old Testament, and Wisdom and Ecclesiasticus in the Apocrypha—takes a variety of forms. The simplest is a couplet of two lines:

> "Righteousness exalts a nation,
>   But sin is a people's ruin." (Prov. 14:34.)

But the proverb may extend to three, four, five, six, or eight lines. Or our practical philosopher may discuss his theme at almost any length, and even give it the form of an ode in praise of Wisdom, as for example in Prov. 1:20–33, which begins

> "Wisdom cries aloud in the streets,
> She lifts up her voice in the squares";

or Prov., ch. 2, the whole of which is devoted to the Blessings of Wisdom. The greatest of such pieces is the Praise of Wisdom in ch. 28 of the great dramatic poem of Job.

Proverbs, like the Psalter, is a collection of collections, and may be read as such. We may begin with the oldest part, or The Words of the Wise, 22:17 to 24:22, the Wisdom of Amen-em-ope, which we have seen was written in Egypt between 1000 and 600 B.C. and was translated into Hebrew probably by Jewish exiles who found refuge in Egypt in the sixth century before Christ. We may group with it its appendix, 24:23–34, "Further Words of the Wise."

We may then proceed to the next oldest section of Proverbs, 10:1 to 22:16, probably written in the times of subjection to Persia, 538–333 B.C.

Then we may read the next preceding part, chs. 1 to 9, which were written in Ptolemaic times, the last three centuries before Christ, and principally in the third century B.C.

Chapters 25 to 29 form a group entitled "The Proverbs of Solomon." They are of varying lengths, from the couplet up:

> "Let another man praise you, and not your own mouth—
> A stranger, and not your own lips." (Prov. 27:2.)

Chapters 30 and 31 are of especial interest for the strange and possibly foreign sages who are mentioned: Agur, from Massa, perhaps in Arabia, 30:1–33, and Lemuel, King of Massa, 31:1–9. The rest of ch. 31 preserves that wonderful tribute to the good wife, which is the finest acrostic poem in the Old Testament, 31:10–31:

> "Her children rise up, and bless her—
> Her husband also, and praises her:
> "Many women have done well,
> But you have excelled them all." (Prov. 31:28, 29.)

The Book of Proverbs reached completion in the third century before Christ, probably toward the year 200.

ECCLESIASTES

The philosophy of the Hebrew wise men found further expression about 150 B.C. in the curious·Book of Ecclesiastes, a Greek word meaning "Preacher," by which the ancient Greek translators sought to convey the meaning of the Hebrew name Koheleth, under which the book was written. Koheleth is plainly a way of saying Solomon, and claiming his authority for the views advanced in the book.

Ecclesiastes is the strangest book in the Bible, for it is sheer utter despondency and bleak pessimism. Life is mere futility and fruitless effort.

> "What does a man gain from all his toil
> At which he toils beneath the sun?" (Eccles. 1:3.)

All nature is mere futile repetition, and there is nothing new under the sun. The poem with which the book begins is a brilliant putting of the pessimist's case, which is documented by the prose paragraphs that follow, chs. 1 and 2. Even learning offers no real satisfaction; increase of knowledge is simply increase of sorrow, 1:18.

And yet the Preacher sees that this is an orderly world, 3:1–8. There is a time for everything under the sun:

> "A time to weep, and a time to laugh; . . .
> A time to keep, and a time to throw away; . . .
> A time to keep quiet, and a time to talk;
> A time to love, and a time to hate;
> A time for war, and a time for peace."

More prose philosophizings follow, on man's limitations, and his merely animal existence, 3:9 to 4:16. But he begins to see man's need of society: "Two are better than one, for they get a good wage for their toil; and if they fall, the one can lift up his companion." (Eccles. 4:9, 10.) He feels that one must fear God, 5:1–9, but still the ruthless man has all the advantage, he declares.

Business success offers no real satisfaction; the laborer's sleep is sweeter than the rich man's. And sometimes money is a curse to its possessor, or it is lost in speculation, and a man must leave his son a pauper. (There is no doubt the Preacher had observed widely, if not deeply.)

This poem on money and the sad fact that you cannot take it with you, 5:10–17, is followed by a prose moral; rich or poor, enjoy your work and bear your lot; that is the gift of God.

The Preacher is no stranger to frustration: "What advantage has the wise man over the fool?" he bitterly inquires. Man is helpless before Fate, ch. 6. Indeed, the Preacher is very much the fatalist: to do it justice he resorts again to poetry in ch. 7:

> "Better is sorrow than laughter, . . .
> Better is the end of a thing than its beginning." (Eccles. 7:3, 8.)

Wisdom is all very well if you have money:

> "Wisdom with an inheritance is good, . . .
> And the advantage of knowledge is that wisdom preserves the
>   life of its owner.
> Behold the work of God;
> For who can straighten out what he has made crooked?
> In the day of prosperity, be joyful,
> And on the day of adversity, consider;
> God has made one thing to balance another." (Eccles. 7:11–14.)

So the Preacher had even discovered the Law of Compensation. He falls back on the fear of God and the cultivation of wisdom, which he says makes a wise man stronger than the ten rulers who are in the city, 7:18, 19. But he has no faith in women, for while he has found one man out of a thousand, he has not found one woman. The truth is, "God made mankind upright, but they have sought out many contrivances." (Eccles. 7:29.)

Ecclesiastes must be read to be appreciated, and many a modern will be amazed at its modernity. The Preacher knows that it will be well with those who fear God, 8:12, and yet life is an empty thing, 9:9.

Wisdom is better than strength, better than weapons of war, and yet one sinner destroys much good, 9:16, 18. Cast your bread upon the waters, for after many days you will find it, 11:1.

"In the morning sow your seed,
And till the evening give your hand no rest;
For you know not which shall prosper, this or that,
Or whether both alike shall be good." (Eccles. 11:6.)

The Preacher ends with a final poem on old age and death which certainly takes a high place in literature, 11:9 to 12:8; but the poem ends as the book began, by declaring it all futile and vain. The little prose epilogue, 12:9–13 (for most of Ecclesiastes is prose), admits the value of such books, 12:11, while scornful of libraries: "Of the making of many books there is no end, and much study is a weariness of the flesh." The disillusioned meditation closes on a moral note: "Fear God and keep his commands."

The Preacher had never felt the fascination of the pursuit of truth in history, or philosophy, or science; he had not been kindled by the splendid possibilities of helping and serving his fellow men; and his religion had brought him no sense of the love of God, and the Great Companion. Like all pessimists, he was a selfish and self-centered man.

THE APOCRYPHA

All the great Bibles, Greek, Latin, German, and English from Coverdale down, have included the books of the Apocrypha, Jewish religious works written mostly in Greek, and except parts of II Esdras between 200 B.C. and A.D. 100.

ECCLESIASTICUS

Early in the second century before Christ there lived in Jerusalem a remarkable man named Jeshua, son of Sirach.

He must have been a leading citizen of the old city; he went out to large dinners, he traveled widely, he observed shrewdly and yet kindly. He loved nature and had a sense of beauty; at the same time he saw deeply into the meaning of work and saw that the farmer and the craftsman supported the fabric of the world, and their prayer was in the practice of their trade. He felt the beauty of the Temple services as no one had done before. We would call him a churchgoer. At the same time, he was religiously devoted to the pursuit of Wisdom, and over many years recorded his keen observations in philosophic verse. It has come down to us in the Apocrypha of the Old Testament, in a Greek translation, made by Jeshua's grandson, about 130 B.C.

The Greeks, who named the books of the Bible for us, called his Wisdom Ecclesiasticus, just why has never been determined. It is the longest of the books of Wisdom, either in the Old Testament or in the Apocrypha. It has a high sense of the physician's calling, and pays a fine tribute to doctors, 38:1–15:

> "Show the physician due honor in view of your need of him,
> For the Lord has created him;
> Healing comes from the Most High,
> And he will receive presents from the king.
> The skill of the physician exalts him,
> And he is admired among the great.
> The Lord has created medicines out of the earth,
> And a sensible man will not refuse them." (Ecclus. 38:1–4.)

Jeshua goes on to pay tribute to the farmer, the builder, the engraver, the painter, the smith, and the potter, 34:25–34, and with them he contrasts the student and the sage, 39:1–11:

"It is not so with the man who applies himself,
And studies the Law of the Most High. . . .
Nations will repeat his wisdom,
And the congregation will utter his praise."

(Ecclus. 39:1, 10.)

Many a practical hint in Jeshua's book has a modern sound. He has advice to masters of ceremonies at large dinners, and to after-dinner speakers at such occasions:

"Speak concisely; say much in few words;
Act like a man who knows more than he says." (Ecclus. 32:8.)
"Prepare what you have to say, and then you will be listened to."
(Ecclus. 33:4.)
"If they make you master of the feast, do not be uplifted;
Behave like one of them among them.
Look after them, and then take your seat." (Ecclus. 32:1.)

Clearly Jeshua was no pessimist, hermit, or misanthrope. He also had his ideas about good manners at dinners:

"Do not rebuke your neighbor at a banquet,
And do not despise him in his mirth.
Do not say a reproachful word to him,
And do not press him to repay you." (Ecclus. 31:31.)
"Be ashamed to lean on your elbow at table." (Ecclus. 41:19.)

Jesus, we remember, had some criticisms to offer of Jewish behavior at such dinners, Luke 14:1–24.

In 42:15 to 43:33 Jeshua describes the glory of God in creation and his little psalm is no mere echo of earlier treatments of that theme.

A still more extended unit in Ecclesiasticus is chs. 44 to 50, the Praise of Famous Men. The opening lines of it are the most familiar in all the Apocrypha:

"Let us now praise distinguished men,
Our forefathers before us. . . .
Peoples will recite their wisdom,
And the congregation declare their praise!"

(Ecclus. 44:1, 15.)

But it is impossible to summarize the Wisdom of Jeshua, the son of Sirach. It is an extraordinary picture of life in Jerusalem in 200 to 175 B.C., a remarkable self-portrait of a leading resident there, alive to every side of life, social, civil, intellectual, religious, in the generation before the Maccabæan uprising threw off the Syrian yoke and made the Jews for a century a free people.

THE WISDOM OF SOLOMON

The conflict between Greek and Jewish ways of life and thought more than once came to a crisis in Alexandria, where both groups were strong and active, and involved the Jews in bitter persecution. Out of such an experience sprang the so-called Wisdom of Solomon, a spirited poem of protest against persecution and of cheer for the victims of it. It called for steadfastness in the face of persecution and denounced those who took refuge in apostasy. It further went on to show the folly of idolatry, so rife in Alexandria, with its huge Serapeum, one of the two greatest buildings in that ancient world.

Over against Ecclesiastes, with its Epicurean tendencies, Wisdom looks beyond this life to immortality and sometimes seems even to be correcting views that Ecclesiastes expressed. Ecclesiastes says, 1:11:

"There is no memory of earlier people,
And likewise of later people who shall be,
There will be no memory with those who are later still."

But Wisdom says ungodly men (1:16) say such things as

"In time our name will be forgotten,
And no one will remember what we have done."
                                        (Wisd. of Sol. 2:4.)

The writer of Wisdom lays hold of the hope of immortality to cheer his persecuted brethren in their trying situation. The persecution of Alexandrian Jews set in motion by the Roman governor Flaccus in A.D. 38 probably called forth the first edition of the book, 1:1 to 11:4. In it the writer sets forth the difference between the upright men who are suffering persecution and their wicked persecutors, with their materialistic view of life:

"Let us lie in wait for the upright, . . .
Let us condemn him to a shameful death."
                                        (Wisd. of Sol. 2:12, 20.)

In a splendid passage the writer sets forth the true view of the situation. The persecutors were wrong; their wickedness blinded them:

"For God created man for immortality,
And made him the image of his own eternity, . . .
The souls of the upright are in the hand of God.
And no torment can reach them. . . .
But they are at peace. . . .
Their hope is full of immortality."
                                        (Wisd. of Sol. 2:23; 3:1, 3, 4.)

The fate of the Jewish martyrs awakens the writer to the great idea that a short life nobly spent may be more significant than a long one:

> "Being perfected in a little while he has fulfilled long years,
> For his soul pleased the Lord." (Wisd. of Sol. 4:13, 14.)

Their persecutors will leave no more impression than a bird's flight through the empty air:

> "But the upright live forever,
> And their reward is with the Lord,
> And the Most High takes care of them." (Wisd. of Sol. 5:15.)

This first part of Wisdom, chs. 1 to 5, concludes with a spirited picture of God in full armor rising to the defense of his people, 5:15–23. The reader will be struck with the resemblance to Eph. 6:14–17.

The persecution, with its victims and its instigators, is the theme of chs. 1 to 5. Then the writer turns to the duties of kings and rulers, 6:1 to 11:4, recommending that they cultivate Wisdom. Assuming the character of Solomon, he declares his devotion to Wisdom, and declares her supreme value. The writer's view of Wisdom is broader than that of his predecessors, for it has room for something of science too:

> "The constitution of the world and the working of the elements; . . .
> The cycles of the years and the positions of the stars,
> The natures of animals, and the dispositions of wild beasts, . . .
> The varieties of plants and the virtues of roots."
>
> (Wisd. of Sol. 7:17, 19, 20.)

The reader will observe that the occasional personification of Wisdom in chs. 1 to 6 gives way in 7:1 to 11:4 to the use of the word almost as a name for God himself. The description of it reaches its climax in 7:25, 26:

> "For she is the breath of the power of God,
> And a pure emanation of his almighty glory;
> Therefore nothing defiled can enter into her.
> For she is a reflection of the everlasting light,
> And a spotless mirror of the activity of God,
> And a likeness of his goodness."

Solomon's prayer for Wisdom in ch. 9 is evidently suggested by the account in I Kings 3:5–9. The writer then tells how Wisdom guided the progress of mankind from Adam to Moses, 10:1 to 11:4.

The rest of the book is clearly the work of another, less gifted, hand. It was probably written a little later than the first part, to meet the situation created by the demand for divine honors made by the Emperor Gaius in A.D. 40. That will explain the polemic against idolatry that pervades these chapters. The Jews had been called upon to worship the emperor's image:

> "By the orders of monarchs carved images were worshiped. . . .
> They imagined how they looked, far away,
> And made a visible image of the king they honored."
>
> (Wisd. of Sol. 14:16, 17.)

The main idea of the writer of the second part of the book, 11:5 to 19:22, is that the very things that helped the Hebrews became the means of punishing their persecutors. This he elaborates and reiterates, reveling in intricacies and artificialities, until the reader is worn out. The second part of the book thus presents a painful contrast to the first, which deserves all the fine things that have been said of it. The original book, Wisdom 1:1 to 11:4, is in fact the brightest gem of Alexandrian Jewish literature.

Twenty years later Paul quoted Wisdom in Colossians, 1:5, and it seems to have been in his mind when he wrote Romans. The author of Hebrews quotes it in beginning his epistle, finding in Christ the embodiment of God's wisdom: "He is the reflection of God's glory, and the representation of his being." Compare Wisdom 7:26 quoted above. Finally, in identifying the Wisdom of God and the Word of God as embodied in Jesus, the Gospel of John is probably guided by Wisdom 9:1, 2, and 9:

> "Who created all things by your word,
> And by your wisdom formed man. . . .
> And with you is wisdom, which knows your works,
> And was present when you made the world."

Read chs. 1 to 5 for the picture of the Alexandrian persecution and its martyrs. Then read 6:1 to 11:4, on the worth of wisdom, especially to all kings and rulers, from Solomon down. And finally, the strange appendix, 11:5 to 19:22, on the extraordinary providence of God, in using the same instruments to bless his people and punish their enemies.

CHAPTER FIFTEEN

Dramatic Poetry

WHILE THE Hebrew genius did not develop drama in the strict Greek sense of the word, the Old Testament preserves two great poems that are so essentially dramatic in structure that they cannot be understood as anything else. They contain little or no action, consisting entirely of songs or speeches. In theme, they are as different as two books can be, for they are The Book of Job and The Song of Songs.

JOB

The subject of The Book of Job is the problem of human suffering. The situation is briefly sketched in prose at the beginning, chs. 1 and 2, and at the end, 42:7–16. These passages present the story of an upright man who through no fault of his was overwhelmed with misfortune, but was ultimately restored to prosperity and happiness—clearly a piece of fiction, for the man is described as perfectly upright. The story may be, and indeed probably is, older than the poem, and will be dealt with in Chapter Sixteen on "Fiction." But it has been made the framework of a philosophical debate on the problem of the suffering which upright people are so often called upon to endure. What can it mean?

138

For the prevalent view among the Hebrews was that calamity and misfortune were the consequences of wrongdoing, and revealed the fact that anyone overtaken by them must be guilty of some offense against God's laws. To the pain of the misfortune was therefore added the disapproval of one's friends and acquaintances, which of course enhanced and embittered it. The problem of Job is, Can this really be the will of God, when so often the punishment seems out of all proportion to the fault?

Somewhat in the manner of a Greek dialog the case is argued by the holders of the opposing views. First the stage is set, chs. 1 and 2, in prose, but with the principal speeches in poetry. Job is to be tried to the utmost; God believes that he will stand the test.

Job loses his property, his children, and his health. His leprosy is the last straw. Three of his old friends gather about him to comfort him, but he is so changed they do not know him. They break into bitter lamentation; then they sit down with him on the ground for seven days and nights in silence, which is at last broken by Job himself, as he lifts up his voice in sublime despair to curse the day he was born, ch. 3.

Was there ever such rhetoric as that of The Book of Job? It fairly overwhelms the reader like a huge wave. Its insight, its imagery, its wealth of symbols, its power of expression, its depth of feeling sweep on in unabated flood through forty pages, unmatched in literature. The modern reader accustomed to writing of less power and more restraint can hardly stand up against this tide of eloquence. Fortunately it is broken into a series of speeches, by Job and his friends. Job's friends seek to justify his situation as something he has somehow deserved, but Job protests his innocence.

Eliphaz speaks, and Job replies, chs. 4 to 7; Bildad speaks, and Job replies, chs. 8 to 10; Zophar speaks, and Job replies, chs. 11 to 14. Then in a second cycle of speeches, Eliphaz speaks again and Job replies, chs. 15 to 17; Bildad speaks again, and Job replies, chs. 18 and 19; Zophar speaks again and Job replies, chs. 20 and 21. In a third cycle, Eliphaz speaks a third time, and Job replies, chs. 22 to 24; Bildad speaks a third time, and Job replies, 25:1 to 27:6; and Zophar apparently (although his name is not repeated) speaks a third time, and utters also a hymn of praise to Wisdom (ch. 28), and Job replies, 27:7 to 31:40. In ch. 31 his words reach a tremendous climax as he protests his uprightness in all the relations of life, and cries out to God for justice.

A curious interlude now follows, probably inserted in Job a century or more after it was written, to uphold the position of Job's friends that Job must, after all, have committed sins that have merited this punishment, whether he is aware of them or not. A man named Elihu breaks into the debate with four speeches, chs. 32 to 37. Elihu's eloquence is hardly equal to that of his seniors, however, and they pay no attention whatever to what he says, although he pauses occasionally to give them an opportunity to reply.

But Job's wild words, at the end of ch. 31:

> "O that one would listen to me!
> Here is my signature! Let the Almighty answer me!"

really introduce God's reply, which begins with ch. 38:

> "Then the Lord answered Job from the whirlwind, saying,
> 'Who is this that obscures counsel
> By words without knowledge?
> Gird up, now, your loins like a man,
> That I may question you, and do you instruct me.'"

The Lord's speech is a magnificent account of God in nature, his power and wisdom. To me this seems the most sublime part of the whole book. It is a bold series of rhetorical questions:

> "Where were you when I laid the foundations of the earth? . . .
> Who enclosed the sea with doors, . . .
> And said, 'Thus far shall you come and no farther,
> And here shall your proud waves be stayed'?
> Have you ever in your life commanded the morning?
> Or assigned its place to the dawn, . . .
> Can you bind the chains of the Pleiades,
> Or loosen the girdle of Orion? . . .
> Can you give strength to the horse? . . .
> As often as the trumpet sounds he says 'Aha';
> And smells the battle from afar,
> The thunder of the captains and the war-cry."
> (Job 38:4, 8, 11, 12; 39:19, 25.)

Job replies; he has no more to say, 40:3–5, and the Lord speaks again, out of the tempest. He tells of those wonders of creation, the hippopotamus and the crocodile. Job replies:

> "I had heard of thee by the hearing of the ear;
> But now my eye has seen thee.
> Therefore I retract and repent,
> In dust and ashes." (Job 42:5, 6.)

But the magnificence of The Book of Job as literature must not distract us from its religious message. Job's problem is left unsolved. It remains a grave question why so many good and earnest people suffer misfortune and bereavement and loss, for no apparent reason. It only appears that in the infinite wisdom and goodness of God, there must be an explanation for it, although our minds cannot fathom it. And this is after all simply the Christian doctrine of faith, which does not demand an explanation of every experience but through good and ill fortune alike puts its trust in God's love and care. It was not so much disaster that had prostrated Job as the fearful thought that God had forsaken him; but when God speaks to him he is satisfied. His inner experience of God convinces him that there is a meaning in life beyond all that we can see.

As you read Job cycle by cycle, yield yourself to its far-off oriental imagery, of Arab encampments and caravans, tenting under the desert stars, with traveler's tales of Egypt and the wonders of the distant Nile; not forgetting to grapple with Job with the great personal religious problem with which he struggled. Remember that it is a great debate, and that the writer is more than half the time presenting views with which he disagrees, so that even Job himself is not wholly right.

THE SONG OF SONGS

The only other actual piece of drama in the Bible, The Song of Songs, is as different from The Book of Job as it can be, for it deals not with observation, introspection, and reflection but with pure emotion. It is the one love poem in the Old Testament, and preserves the songs which the common people in Jewish villages sang when young people got married. We must class it as drama because, although they are not named, different people evidently sang the songs, as the contents of the various songs reveal. Just as we now proclaim a girl "queen" of some celebration for a day or a week, they playfully called the bridegroom "king" of the wedding week, and as Solomon was the most splendid of kings, he is "Solomon," for the period of the festivities. This is the key to the strange designation of the bride, as Shulammith, which is simply the feminine form of Shelomoh, the Hebrew name of Solomon. As he is Shelomoh, she is Shulammith. The names are much more alike in Hebrew than any translation indicates.

The Song of Songs means the finest of songs, and as Solomon was famed in Hebrew tradition as their greatest song writer—I Kings 4:32 credits him with five thousand—it was ascribed to him. But it is most clearly a group of songs, a song made up of songs, the bride and bridegroom alternating with the chorus of villagers.

The bride rejoices in her lover's affection, Song of Songs 1:2–4. She and he exchange compliments, 1:7 to 2:2. The bride acknowledges her attachment to him, 2:3 to 3:5. The bridegroom, enthroned upon the threshing sledge, is cheered by the townsfolk, 3:6–11:

> "What is this coming up from the wilderness, . . .
> Ah, it is the litter of Solomon. . . .
> O daughters of Jerusalem, go forth,
>   and gaze upon King Solomon, . . .
>   on the day of his nuptials." (Song 3:6, 7, 11.)

With characteristic oriental frankness, the groom enlarges upon the bride's charms, 4:1–15; the bride confesses her love, 4:16; 5:2–8, and describes the bridegroom's attractions, 5:10–16. The bridegroom responds with renewed compliments, 6:4–10. All the women and girls are asking who she is:

> "Who is she that breaks forth like the dawn,
>   as beautiful as the moon?"

As the bride dances the sword dance, the onlookers describe her physical attractions in the most outspoken terms, 6:13 to 7:6. Then in a final series of interchanges, now and then interrupted by the chorus of villagers, the bride and groom renew their protestations of love and devotion, 7:7 to 8:14.

Read in this way, the Song is full of interest as a picture of ancient Hebrew village life, and its natural interest in happy marriage. Jews and Christians have both sought to find religious allegories in the Song, but such meanings are clearly imported into it. It is not strange that we possess one secular Hebrew poem, and that it should deal with a matter of such universal interest as love and marriage. A wedding was not a religious ceremony among the Hebrews; the groom simply went to the bride's house, accompanied by his friends, and brought the bride in joyous procession to his house, in token of the fact that she was now his wife. A feast of a week or more ensued, if his means permitted.

The interpretation of the various parts of the Song in this way is confirmed by the fact that in Syria such things are still customary among the peasantry; the wedding procession, the bride's sword dance, accompanied by the description of her charms sung by the onlookers, the bride and groom honored for the following week as king and queen, enthroned above the threshing floor. Modern residents in Syria still find these things practiced among the villages.

The Song of Songs preserves one of the most beautiful of spring songs:

> "Rise, my love,
>   my beautiful one, come away;

For, see, the winter is past,
the rain is over and gone;
The flowers have appeared on the earth,
the time of song has come;
And the call of the turtle dove
is heard in our land." (Song 2:10–12.)

As you read it, listen for the changing singers, the girl, the lover, and their friends the villagers, as they in turn take up the wedding song.

CHAPTER SIXTEEN

Fiction

IN ADVANCING the interests of religion, the Hebrew genius
did not neglect the possibilities of fiction. Even the fable,
perhaps the most rudimentary form of fiction, appears now
and then in the Bible. Back in the days of the Judges, Jotham,
fleeing for his life from his brutal brother Abimelech, paused
on top of Mount Gerizim to shout to the men of Shechem the
fable of the Trees Electing a King, Judg. 9:8–20. II Kings
records how a king of Israel once answered a declaration of
war from the king of Judah with the fable of the Thistle and
the Cedar. It is one of the shortest of fables:

"The thistle that was in Lebanon sent to the cedar which
was in Lebanon, saying, 'Give your daughter to my son as
wife.' But a wild beast that was in Lebanon passed by and
trampled down the thistle." (II Kings 14:9.)

What he meant was that he was too proud to fight. But
as the king of Judah insisted upon it, the king of Israel defeated and despoiled him.

A truer form of fiction is found in the parables or illustra-
tive stories that the prophets sometimes used, to bring home
their teachings to their hearers. Such was the story the Prophet
Nathan so courageously told King David, who had caused
Uriah the Hittite to be killed in battle so that David could

take Uriah's wife. It is the story of the poor man's little ewe lamb, in II Sam., ch. 12, and is from any point of view one of the great parables. The ewe lamb has become a symbol in the world's literature.

Isaiah's Song of the Vineyard, the carefully tended vineyard that produced wild grapes, 5:1–7, is a poetical parable. But these parables and fables will be read as parts of the books in which they appear. We must think of the *books* of the Bible which are fiction, that is, short stories.

The Book of Job is more than a novel, for it is principally drama and debate, but its setting is unmistakably fiction. It deals with a vague figure, not of Israel at all, but a patriarch of Edom, of such perfection of character as no man had ever achieved, for he was perfect and upright; he feared God and shunned wickedness. Indeed, God himself is described as pointing him out to Satan as a perfect man. This must at once inform every reader that he is an ideal figure, and the setting of the drama is religious fiction.

RUTH

Job belongs to the early part of the fourth century before Christ and from the same period comes the first extended piece of prose fiction in the Bible, the idyl of Ruth. It took form in the days when Ezra's protest against Jews marrying outsiders had compelled the casting off of wives of heathen parentage, with their children, certainly a cruel and unnatural proceeding for any husband. Against such decrees, the story of Ruth, hardly four pages long, tells how in the days of the Judges a man of Judah, in accordance with Jewish law, had married the widow of one of his kinsmen, although she was a woman of Moab, and not of Judah; and how from that marriage, in the third generation, had sprung David the king. It is a short story with a purpose, and a most important one, for it is a voice raised in later Judaism against the narrow nationalism that was so disastrous. It stands in the Bible just after Judges, because its scene is laid in the times of the Judges.

JONAH

At the other end of the Old Testament, tucked away among the Minor Prophets, is the greatest and one of the shortest of all short stories, the story of Jonah. Everybody knows it; no one will ever forget it. What is sad about it is that the point of it is generally overlooked. The writer's vehicle has overshadowed his intention. It has run away with it.

Jonah is much more than a wonder story. It is meant to arrest Jewish attention and fix it upon the truth that God cares for other people besides the Jews, and that their habit of meeting bitterness with bitterness, which of course only intensified the other's bitterness, was not the will of God. His will was pardon, forgiveness, and love, even for one's enemies.

Jonah belonged to the Northern Kingdom, which was destroyed by the Assyrians from Nineveh in 721 B.C. But God calls Jonah to go and preach against Nineveh. Instead of obeying, he goes in the opposite direction and gets aboard a ship bound for the other end of the Mediterranean. Rescued miraculously from the sailors, the storm, and the fish, and summoned again to his task, he obeys, and calls on the Ninevites to repent or be destroyed. He hoped that they would be destroyed, but to his great disappointment they repent.

Greatly disheartened by his success, Jonah makes himself

a shelter near the city and prays for death. God speaks to him and tells him that he pities Nineveh, with its thousands of helpless children. So God's favor is not something to be hoarded and enjoyed, but something to be shared with other men and other peoples, even one's enemies. Jonah is the first missionary book in the world. If people would recognize it as fiction, they might get from it its meaning, which was never more needed than today.

TOBIT

As time went on, after the work of Alexander the Great, and the Greek way of life, which seemed to the Jews so secular, became more and more prevalent in Syria and Egypt, a Jew in Egypt wrote the story of the ideal Jew. He did not want his nation's patterns of life to be forgotten or overshadowed by those of the Greeks that were so dominant in Egypt under the Ptolemies. Greek art, Greek literature, Greek speech, Greek thought, and Greek religion were immensely in vogue, and Jews were strongly tempted to adopt them. Something must be done in Greek to recall attention to Jewish ideals of living. So some unknown Jew wrote in Greek the story of Tobit, in our Apocrypha.

The story is set far back in the eighth century before Christ, before the fall of the Northern Kingdom of Israel. Tobit belonged to it, for he lived in Galilee, but he remained loyal to Jerusalem and went there for the Passover every year, taking not just a tithe, a tenth, but three-tenths of his year's income, to distribute. With the rest of the Israelites he is carried off into captivity in Nineveh, where he rises to wealth, becoming the king's buyer. But under Sennacherib he loses favor, chiefly because of his pious practice of burying the bodies of Jews put to death by the king. His fortunes rise and fall; his devotion to the Law leads to his blindness, he is poor, and his only support is what his wife can earn. But he quarrels with her, and the poor old fellow longs for death.

Then he remembers a sum of money he had deposited in the times of his prosperity with a friend in Ragae in Media, and he sends his son Tobias to get it. What happened to this young man, the real hero of the story; who escorted him on his journey; how he found the girl of his dreams and under what hair-raising circumstances he married her, and came home again, must be read to be appreciated. Tobit is a romance, varied and colorful, and still influences English literature. No doubt it helped to keep many a Jew from wandering off into Greek views and habits. It is twenty pages long and can be read in an hour.

Tobit was not the only effort made by Greek-speaking Jews of Egypt to promote interest in Jewish history and culture among the Greeks about them. About the middle of the second century before Christ, stimulated by the deliverance of Jerusalem from the Syrians and the renewal of the Temple worship under Judas Maccabæus in 165 B.C., a Jew in Egypt wrote in Greek I Esdras, an imaginative account of what Ezra had done to restore Judaism in Jerusalem, more than two hundred years before. He mingles the narratives of Ezra and Nehemiah in strange ways, and gets his Persian kings badly mixed, but about the only new thing he relates is the story of the Three Guardsmen in the bed chamber of Darius, I Esdras, chs. 3 and 4. The story is a beautiful bit of folklore, but we must consider it in Chapter Seventeen as a part of the later history in which it is preserved.

DANIEL

To the same general period, the emancipation of Judah from Syrian control, belongs also The Book of Daniel. In Judea the struggle with Hellenism—the effort to impose Greek ways upon the Jews—had been acute. The king of Syria, enthusiastic for Greek culture, regarded his Jewish subjects as a backward, unenlightened people, and sought to force Greek civilization upon them in place of their Law and worship. It was this that called forth the Maccabæan uprising. The Pious party that formed about the Maccabæan leaders went through great tribulation during their persecution by the Syrians who were trying to Hellenize them. Daniel was written to fortify them in their struggle. It told how long before, in the days of the Exile, Daniel and his Jewish friends had stood firm against the demands of an idolatrous king and by their patience and fortitude had at last prevailed.

The last six chapters of Daniel, 7 to 12, present a series of apocalyptic visions, which are not to be viewed as fiction, and must be read with other apocalypses, Enoch, II Esdras, and the Revelation of John. But chs. 1 to 6 form an extraordinary series of stories, designed to encourage the Pious party in its resistance to the cruel demands the Syrians were making upon them. The things they went through can be gathered from the pages of I and II Maccabees.

These stories are so familiar that they need only to be mentioned. Daniel and his friends in exile are chosen to be educated in Chaldean learning, but they refuse to eat heathen food (just as the adherents of the Maccabees were doing); what came of it? (Ch. 1.) Nebuchadnezzar the king has a

mysterious dream; only Daniel can interpret it, ch. 2. Daniel's
three friends, Shadrach, Meshach, and Abednego, refuse to
worship the idol set up by the king and are thrown into a fiery
furnace, but escape, ch. 3. Nebuchadnezzar has a dream, which
Daniel reluctantly interprets as meaning that the king will
have an attack of madness, and this comes to pass, ch. 4. King
Belshazzar gives a great feast for all his court, but in the
midst of it a hand appears and writes upon the wall four
mysterious words; only Daniel can interpret them; they pronounce the doom of Belshazzar's kingdom, and that night
Darius the Mede takes the city, ch. 5. Then, in the most famous
story of all this dramatic series, Daniel, who has become
Darius' prime minister, is thrown into the den of lions because he continues to pray regularly to God, ch. 6. Everyone
knows the outcome.

These are the immortal stories with which the persecuted
Jews of Judah cheered one another in their time of persecution. They were written partly in Hebrew, the old literary
language, and partly in Aramaic, the vernacular, which everybody understood. The writer was evidently at home in both,
and hardly knew when he passed from one to the other.
Certainly the Fiery Furnace, Belshazzar's Feast, and the Den
of Lions are among the most famous and familiar stories in
the world.

ESTHER

To the same general period, toward 150 B.C., belongs the
romantic story of Esther, the Jewish girl who became a queen,
and once when her people were in peril heroically came to
their rescue. The Book of Esther stands after Ezra and

Nehemiah, for like them it deals with the Persian period of Jewish history. The scene is laid in the time of Xerxes, who has dismissed his wife Vashti and is looking for a new queen. Mordecai, Esther's uncle, directs her to join the applicants, and she is chosen by the king and becomes queen. In that position and, directed by Mordecai, she is able to thwart a plot to destroy the Jews all over the Persian Empire, and the instigator of the plot is put to death. The story closes with the institution of a new Jewish feast to celebrate this national deliverance, the feast of Purim, and it was probably to promote the acceptance of this feast by the Jews that Esther was written. Xerxes reigned from 486 to 465 B.C., but we cannot trace the observance of Purim before the middle of the second century before Christ, and Esther was probably written then. In fact, Purim was probably a Persian feast that the Jews in Persia adopted. The names of the characters in the story correspond to those of Babylonian religion, Esther to Ishtar, Mordecai to Marduk, and so on.

Esther is, in short, a great piece of Jewish fiction, intended to accomplish a definite effect in popularizing a new feast among the Jews of Palestine. Purim was a secular feast, when the Jews gave dinners for their friends and made presents to one another.

Half a century later Esther appeared in Greek in a new and enlarged edition. Some Jew in Egypt was evidently shocked that Esther made no mention of God or prayer, and he sought to supply these omissions. Dreams, decrees, and prayers are now scattered through the book, increasing its size by about half. It is in this enlarged and more religious form that Esther appears in the Apocrypha and in the Greek Bible.

JUDITH

Of all these great old stories, none really surpasses the story of Judith. It was written by a member of the new Pharisaic party, who felt deeply the importance of keeping every bit of Jewish Law, in any and all circumstances. It may have been written in Hebrew about 150 B.C., but if so it was soon translated into Greek, and it is in Greek that it has come down to us. It tells the exciting story of a beautiful Jewish widow who, when her city was besieged by the Assyrians, induced the Assyrian general to let her take refuge in his tent. When he had fallen into a drunken sleep, she slew him with his own sword and thus delivered her city from its foes. It reminds you of Jael and Sisera, in the book of Judges (4:21), and it has had no little influence in literature and in painting. The book has no historical importance, except in the field of literature; indeed, it cares nothing about history, for in the very first line it describes Nebuchadnezzar as reigning over the Assyrians in Nineveh. But Nebuchadnezzar was king of Babylonia, not Assyria, and his capital was not Nineveh but Babylon.

What the writer does care about is the Law, its fasts and foods, its tithes and its ablutions, and he is at great pains to tell how even in the hostile heathen camp, Judith never forgot the smallest requirements of the Law but carried them out. The modern reader will feel a certain incongruity between her unswerving devotion to her ceremonial duties and her relentless murder of an unconscious man, but perhaps from a literary point of view this is the special genius of the book of Judith. The reader must not forget that for the author, the point of the story was Judith's devotion, even in the most adverse circumstances, to the ceremonial law.

SUSANNA

Early in the first century before Christ, a Jerusalem novelist of the Pharisaic school wrote the story of Susanna. Not long after, it was translated into Greek in Egypt and appended to the Greek version of Daniel. The first English Bibles all called it the Story of Susanna, but the Geneva Bible (1560) and the King James Version (1611) named it the History of Susanna.

Susanna was a beautiful young woman who was married to a prominent Jew in Babylon. Two Jewish elders who were friends of her husband became enamored of her and one day surprised her bathing in her garden. They threatened her, but she resisted their advances. When she called out for help, they declared that they had found a young man with her and were trying to detain him. (You are reminded of Tarquin and Lucrece.) When she was tried, their testimony agreed, and as it was two witnesses against one, she was condemned to be stoned to death.

But on her way to execution, Daniel met them, and protested. How he got her off is one of the classics of legal examination, and the result was that Jewish legal procedure was improved by a provision that perjurers if found out had to be punished, whether anyone had actually been put to death because of their perjury or not. The story of Jesus and the adulterous woman found in old versions of John (7:53 to 8:11) bears a strong resemblance to the story of Susanna.

Shakespeare named his daughters Judith and Susanna, and it is easy to see where he got these beautiful names.

BEL AND THE DRAGON

Dorothy Sayers begins her *First Omnibus of Crime* with two stories from the Apocrypha, Susanna and Bel. Bel is really two short stories under one title, which in the King James Version (1611) read, "The history of the destruction of Bel and the Dragon, cut off from the end of Daniel." They were written in Greek, early in the first century before Christ, by a Jew of Alexandria, to keep the Jews from the idolatry so triumphant there at that time. They were added to the Greek translation of Daniel to form the end of it, when the story of Susanna was placed at the beginning of it, to present Daniel's debut, as we might say. Bel was a huge idol set up by King Cyrus, and Daniel, who must have been very old indeed if he survived until Cyrus' day, was asked by the king why he did not worship it, since it consumed such quantities of flour, oil, and sheep as disappeared every night from its sanctuary. By a skilful piece of detection, Daniel shows the king what actually became of these offerings.

The Dragon was really a huge serpent which the king worshiped, much as such creatures were venerated in Greek and oriental shrines in antiquity. Daniel ingeniously destroys it, and in consequence is once more thrown into the lions' den, where he has a new experience. Bel and the Dragon is perhaps the oldest detective story in the world.

THE PARABLES

We have seen the part fiction played in Old Testament literature and in the Apocrypha. Has it any place in the New Testament? Yes, a most important one, for it was Jesus' favorite and characteristic vehicle. He was not so much moral-

izer and lawgiver as story-teller. His stories we call the
parables, which is just the Greek word for a figure of speech.
The Gospels of Matthew, Mark, and Luke contain in the
neighborhood of forty of them, all of them familiar to all of
us today. Some of them are barely a sentence long: "The
Kingdom of Heaven is like a hoard of money, buried in a
field, which a man found, and buried again. And he was over-
joyed, and went and sold everything he had and bought the
field." "Again, the Kingdom of Heaven is like a dealer in
search of fine pearls. He found one costly pearl, and went and
sold everything he had, and bought it." Matt. 13:44, 45.

The parables of the Sower, Matt. 13:1–23; of the Seed
growing of itself, Mark 4:26–29; of a man's Enemy Sowing
Weeds in the man's field, Matt. 13:24–30; of the Mustard
Seed, Mark 4:30–32, represent one type of parable. But there
are more elaborate ones, such as the three that make up
the twenty-fifth chapter of Matthew, the Bridesmaids, the
Talents, and the Judgment. Each parable is meant to teach a
single great lesson, which it presents with inimitable clearness
and force. The action of the Gospel of Matthew reaches its
climax in the parable of the Vineyard, 21:33–41, as its moral
teaching does in the parable of the Judgment, 25:31–46.

Some of the greatest are found only in Luke—the Rich
Fool, 12:17–21; the Great Supper, 14:16–24; the Prodigal
Son, 15:12–32; the Rich Man and Lazarus, 16:19–31; the
Pharisee and the Tax Collector, 18:10–14; and the Good
Samaritan, 10:30–37, which has recently been called the finest
summary of the spirit of Christianity.

Certainly no one, in the Bible or out of it, has ever em-
ployed the art of fiction with greater effect than Jesus did.

CHAPTER SEVENTEEN

Later Histories

I ESDRAS

THE HISTORICAL interest which had lain dormant in Judaism for a hundred and fifty years after the Chronicler wrote his books, awoke to new life when the stirring exploits of the Maccabees restored the Temple worship in 165 B.C., and began to free their people from foreign domination after more than four hundred years of it. Those were times to awaken great memories of the past, and they stirred one Jewish historian to write in Greek an imaginative account of former restorations and rededications, from the time of Josiah's reformation in 621 B.C. to the acceptance of the Law in 397 B.C. under the leadership of Ezra.

The author was one of those Jews in Egypt who knew Greek and wished to make his people's past achievements known to the Greek world in which he lived. He wrote in good Greek, and based his narrative, not very skilfully, upon what he found in the Hebrew books of Chronicles, Ezra, and Nehemiah. His book was called I Esdras, the Greek form for

Ezra, because he made so much use of The Book of Ezra in composing it. The Jews had just recaptured Jerusalem, rededicated the Temple, and won back the right to observe their beloved Law. I Esdras was written to remind its public that history had been repeating itself, for long before, after the Exile, the Jews had rededicated and reoccupied their Temple, and then in the time of Ezra had accepted and adopted the Law.

The principal addition that the writer makes to his Hebrew sources, aside from the occasional confusion he introduces into it, is a palpable bit of folklore, the story of the Three Guardsmen. Being on duty in the antechamber of King Artaxerxes one night, they fell to debating what was the strongest thing in the world. One proposed Wine, another, the King, and the third, Woman, but added that really Truth was the strongest of all. The king put the question to his courtiers, who decided in favor of Truth, and the third guardsman was told to choose his own reward. He proved to be Zerubbabel, and asked permission to rebuild the Temple.

This story in chs. 3 and 4 is the most spirited part of I Esdras and offers a pleasing contrast to the long list of names of persons or groups who returned from the Exile, reproduced from The Book of Ezra, in chs. 5 and 9. Unfortunately, the writer of I Esdras, in using The Book of Ezra, transposed two sections of that book, putting Ezra 4:7–24 before 2:1 to 4:5, thus making events of the reign of Darius in 520 B.C. follow action taken by Artaxerxes, after 465 B.C.

Yet I Esdras has contributed one immortal line to literature; it is the cry of the Persian courtiers when they voted unanimously for the motion of the third guardsman:

"Truth is mighty and will prevail!"

THE BOOKS OF MACCABEES

The revolt of the Pious party in Judaism against the Hellenizing campaign of their ruler, the king of Syria, led in 165 B.C. to their religious liberty and eventually their political independence. This was the work of three great men, Judas Maccabæus, the military genius of the family, and his two brothers, Jonathan, who succeeded Judas as head of the Jewish people in 160 B.C., and Simon, who followed Jonathan in 143 B.C. Simon was murdered in 135 B.C. and was followed by his son John Hyrcanus, who was high priest as well as governor and general. John ruled for more than thirty years, 135–103 B.C., and was followed by his son Alexander Jannæus. These were the Hasmonæans, and few pages of history can compare in heroic and romantic interest with the chapter they wrote. No wonder some patriotic Jew in the days of Alexander Jannæus, early in the first century before Christ, set out to record the extraordinary series of events that had led to the achievement of what his party had always striven for, political independence.

Even then there were two parties in Judaism, one, the Pious, or Pharisaic, party, which aimed at religious liberty; the other the Hasmonæan or Sadducean party, which aspired to political freedom as well. Judas had recovered the religious liberty of the Jews, but it had remained for Simon to secure their political independence of the Syrian Empire. It is this latter achievement that interests the writer of I Maccabees and leads him to tell its tragic story, for all three of the great Maccabæan brothers died by violence.

While the state papers quoted in the book are of doubtful

authenticity, at least for the dates assigned to them, I Maccabees is in general a valuable historical record of the last great chapter in the history of the Hebrew nation. Its dates are given in the Seleucid era, which reckons from the accession of Seleucus I, King of Syria, in 311 B.C.

II Maccabees is not, as might be supposed, a continuation of I Maccabees, but an account of the first phase of the Maccabæan struggle, written from the Pharisaic point of view. Some Pharisee living in Egypt felt that the story as told in I Maccabees left out God's part in the Jews' success and made it too much a merely human accomplishment. He had no interest in the story beyond the point where the Temple was recovered from the Syrians and rededicated to the worship of God; indeed, he did not follow the story on to the death of Judas. His book covers the years 175–160 B.C., which are covered in I Macc., chs. 1 to 7. The writer claims to base his book on a history of the struggle by Jason of Cyrene, which was probably written about 100 B.C., but has disappeared. But he clearly made use of I Maccabees too.

The Pharisaic color of his book is very plain. He is interested in miracles, angels, and resurrection; that hope makes its first definite appearance here, in the horrible stories of the Maccabæan martyrs in chs. 6 and 7. He is much concerned over Sabbaths, feasts, and Law. But the most significant contrast between his book and I Maccabees is that he ends his story when religious liberty has been attained; he cares nothing about the political freedom in which I Maccabees found the climax of its story. He writes in a labored, stilted style, and his bitter party spirit, sermonic interludes, and lack of taste and restraint repel the reader. Yet II Maccabees is of great importance to the New Testament reader, for it is

a book not just about the Pharisees but by one of their own
number; hence it is an important witness as to their real character. The Pharisees advanced greatly in influence after Alexander's widow, Alexandra, became regent in 76 B.C., and it
was probably between her accession and Pompey's capture of
Jerusalem in 63 B.C. that II Maccabees was written, partly
as a reply to the account given in I Maccabees. Read it for a
self-portrait of the Pharisee a hundred years before the ministry of Jesus.

LUKE'S TWO-VOLUME WORK, THE
GOSPEL AND THE ACTS

When in A.D. 56–57 Paul was returning to Palestine
from the Third Missionary Journey, he was joined at Philippi
by a young Greek physician, who went with him to Jerusalem,
stayed near him during his imprisonment at Cæsarea, and
made with him the historic voyage to Italy so graphically
described in the closing chapters of The Acts. His name was
Luke, and he later became the first Greek to take up the pen
for the new faith.

For as the years went by, and the mission among the
Greeks that Paul had founded and done so much to develop
spread more and more widely, it became clear that the Christian Church was moving toward a great future, and the importance of recording its beginnings before it was too late struck
the Greek mind. Of the work of Paul and his later travels
Luke knew from his travels with Paul and from Paul's own
lips. For the picture of the Early Church in Palestine he had
his own impressions gathered when he had spent two years
there, waiting on Paul during his imprisonment in Cæsarea,

for many primitive Christians would visit that city, and Luke himself would travel far and wide, over a land so rich in religious memories.

But his history must begin with Jesus, and his origin. For this, too, Luke's residence in Palestine and his visits with believers over the land would give him material. Of even more importance was what had been written about Jesus and his ministry and passion by other hands. Certainly Luke had the Gospel of Mark, three-fifths of which he reproduced faithfully in his first volume, which took the form of a new Gospel, that is, an enlargement of Mark, the only Gospel Luke knew. But he could enrich Mark's narrative with other written narratives and accounts of Jesus' teaching, and this he did.

From his account of the Nativity Luke has been called the man who gave us Christmas. But he is also the only one of the Evangelists who gives us any light upon definite dates. He connects the birth of Jesus with the Roman census, Luke 2:1, which usually took place every fourteen years. He dates the beginning of John the Baptist's preaching in Tiberius' fifteenth year, or as we would say A.D. 28–29, Luke 3:1, and says that Jesus was about thirty years old when he began his work.

To Luke we also owe a whole series of the most important and significant of Jesus' parables, as we have seen in considering his first volume as a Gospel side by side with Mark and Matthew. For Luke wrote his history in two volumes, which we know as the Gospel of Luke and The Acts of the Apostles, although he did not give them these names. But he skilfully organized his first volume into something like a biography of Jesus, going back all the way to the announcement of the approaching birth of his forerunner, John the Baptist. His narrative ends with Jesus' promise of the gift of the Spirit to his disciples, the fulfilment of which forms one of the opening events of his second volume, The Acts. It is plain that Luke views Jesus not only as the Messiah of Jewish hope but as the founder of the Christian Church, even more definitely than Matthew had done, for he tells the story of Jesus not only for itself but also as the beginning of the great movement Luke saw already spreading over the Roman world.

It was a forward step of great significance when Christian writers began to plan books of such scope that they required two papyrus scrolls to contain them, that is, books in two volumes. Such a book was Luke-Acts. Acts is so full of interesting narratives that it may at first seem just the story book of early Christianity, but all that it tells serves a purpose and carries the story on toward its goal. The historian shows us the Christian movement breaking through its first narrow Jewish limits to Greek-speaking Jews and proselytes, 6:1–5, Samaritans, 8:1–24, Ethiopians, 9:26–40, Romans, like Cornelius, ch. 10, and finally in Antioch to heathen Greeks, 11:20.

Now Paul comes into the picture, and the mission to the Greeks of the Roman Empire begins. First Cyprus is visited, and the Roman governor believes, 13:4–12. Churches are established in towns of Galatia, in central Asia Minor. On a later journey Paul makes his way all through Asia Minor to Troas, on the shores of the Ægean, and there makes the momentous decision to carry the new faith over into Macedonia and Europe. Luke was perfectly right in the great importance he attached to this step of Paul's, Acts 16:9–12; it was a turning point in Christian history. Paul's missionary travels to Philippi, Thessalonica, Athens, and Corinth, his work in Ephesus on a later journey, his return to Jerusalem, his arrest and imprisonment, his appearances before Jewish and Roman authorities, and finally his adventurous journey to Rome for trial, carry forward the story of the gospel's progress through the ancient world with a rising interest. The book ends with Christianity established in Rome, and being strengthened by the presence there of Paul. And with the gospel planted in the capital of the empire only thirty years after the crucifixion, the Christian future might well appear assured.

Luke was not one of those historians who dealt with reigns and wars, or with gossip and scandal; he saw the value of popular movements and spiritual forces and thought them worth recording for the better understanding of his own generation. In doing this he laid the foundation of church history, for his two-volume book is all that enables us to bridge the gap between Jesus and Paul and to understand how the letters of Paul fit into the rise and progress of Christianity in the first century.

Read Luke's work a volume at a time; the Gospel volume, and then the volume on the march of Christianity through the empire to the capital itself, noting what a veritable torrent of exciting and varied action The Acts is, stripped of its retarding chapter and verse divisions, and cast in an easy, familiar style such as Luke wrote. Its perilous action is interspersed with eloquent speeches in defense of the new faith. It would be hard to find another book of ancient literature which carries the reader so swiftly and naturally through scenes so exciting and significant, set in the splendid cities of the Greco-Roman world, the cities of Jerusalem, Antioch,

Tarsus, Philippi, Thessalonica, Athens, Corinth, Ephesus, Rome.

The Acts may be read in three parts. Chapters 1 to 7 describe the development of the Christian movement in Jerusalem; chs. 8 to 12 tell of its spread to other cities—Samaria, Damascus, Joppa, Cæsarea, and finally Antioch; and chs. 13 to 28 record the work of Paul in carrying the Gospel through Asia Minor and Greece, until he reached Rome itself. Luke was not attempting a life of Paul, though his sketch of him in the second half of The Acts was never equaled. What Luke was really doing was laying the foundation of church history, of which his book is the corner stone.

CHAPTER EIGHTEEN

Letters and Epistles

PERSONAL LETTERS are, it is generally agreed, the most trustworthy kind of historical sources, and in these the New Testament is particularly rich. In fact, Christian literature began with such letters, and their writer, the Apostle Paul, wrote more than one-fifth of the New Testament. When some crisis in one of Paul's churches demanded his attention, it was his habit to meet it with a letter. He was a man of overflowing intellectual and spiritual power, and these letters appear by modern standards extremely long. Many of them are longer than most of the books of the Minor Prophets, and they throw a flood of light upon the life and problems of the Early Church, in the very middle of the first century, A.D. 50 to 62. It has been said of them that they take the roofs off the early Christian meeting places and let us look inside, and this is true. Both for what they contain and for what they have accomplished, they deserve to be called the greatest letters ever written.

Paul was a great thinker, the greatest thinker, we may fairly say, among the writers of the books of the New Testament. Though his letters were called forth by pressing local situations and problems, he dealt with these in a way so broad and penetrating that the great principles he reached are valid and potent still, after almost nineteen hundred years. In Galatians he struck the keynote of democracy and set religion free; in I Corinthians he pointed out the shining path of Christian conduct, controlled by the great principle of love; and in Romans he found in faith the indispensable basis of character and acceptance with God. Twentieth-century thinkers have more than once announced as modern discoveries positions Paul arrived at and proclaimed centuries ago. As a thinker, he deserves serious attention.

I THESSALONIANS

The earliest book of the New Testament, though it was written not as a book but simply as a private letter to a group of friends, is a letter to the Christians at Thessalonica, which Paul wrote in Corinth, in the spring of A.D. 50. He had been forced by the local authorities to leave Thessalonica abruptly, in the midst of his work there, and had proceeded to Athens. He was naturally anxious to know how the little group of Thessalonians who had accepted Christianity had stood the strain of this test of their attachment to their new faith, and so he sent Timothy back to find out, while he went on to Corinth. When Timothy returned and overtook Paul at Corinth, he brought him good news; Paul's sudden departure had not shaken the Thessalonians' new faith; they were steadfast in their Christian allegiance. Paul's relief and joy found expression in this letter, which gives us an excellent view of his relations with his churches. Read this first piece of Christian literature for its picture of the life of hope and mutual affection in the Early Church, and the relations of the missionary to the people.

II THESSALONIANS

A few months later, while Paul was still at Corinth, news reached him from Thessalonica that some of the believers there had gotten the idea that the Day of the Lord had come, and had given up the work by which they made their living, in order to adjust themselves to its demands.

The Old Testament prophecies of the Day of the Lord were often on the lips of early Christians and caused them some confusion of mind, as they sometimes do to Christians today.

To some it seemed that with the appearance of Christ, the Day must have come, and the best way to use what little time remained was to devote it to religious exercises, in preparation for the end. Some of the Thessalonians were possessed with this idea, and so they gave up their usual work as of no further interest or importance. But they became a nuisance and scandal in the Thessalonian church, for they did not devote all their time to their devotions and soon came to be looked upon by their hard-working fellow Christians, who had to support them, as a set of idlers and busybodies.

To correct this situation, Paul wrote his second letter to the Thessalonians, pointing out that the Day of the Lord had not come, for before it came the Antichrist must make his appearance, which must according to Jewish Messianic ideas precede the final coming of the Messiah. Paul sharply corrects the idlers in the church, and points to his own sturdy example of self-support, for he made his living by working at his trade, in order to preach the gospel. He does not hesitate to say, "If a man will not work, give him nothing to eat!"

Read II Thessalonians for its picture of the vivid Messianic expectations of the Early Church, and for its ideal of personal industry and self-support, coupled with readiness to help the really needy.

GALATIANS

Returning to Antioch after a journey that had taken him all the way to Athens and Corinth (the so-called Second Missionary Journey), Paul learned that in his absence of more than two years (A.D. 49–52) a serious mistake of another kind had taken root in the churches he had organized in Galatia. Jewish Christians there had advanced the claim that people not of Jewish blood must accept at least a modified form of Judaism in order to be saved and enter the Christian Church.

Paul saw that this brought with it a return to the old Jewish doctrine of salvation through obedience to the Law, which he knew could not be combined with faith and the life of the Spirit, which were the heart of the Christian experience. Christ had set them free, and they must not go back into bondage.

He immediately wrote the Galatians an impassioned letter, calling upon them to disavow such Jewish teachers and return to the gospel of faith he had preached to them. He claims for himself and his teaching an authority quite independent of the Jewish Christian leaders of Jerusalem, Gal. 1:1 to 2:14. Then, in a kaleidoscopic series of arguments, he points out the flaws in the Judaizers' position, 2:15 to 4:31. The Christian's life is to be governed not by a set of rules but by the Spirit of God which he has received, chs. 5 and 6. If it is, it will exhibit the fruits of the spirit—love, joy, peace, patience, kindness, goodness, faithfulness, gentleness, self-control.

Galatians has been called a charter of religious freedom. It has enduring value in the New Testament, safeguarding Christianity against the dangers of formalism and legalism which in every age threaten its true character as a vital experience of spiritual communion with God and dependence upon him. It is an extraordinary blaze of mingled thought and feeling from beginning to end, almost unparalleled in literature. Read it at a sitting in some vigorous translation that lets its fiery vehemence appear, and see how Paul liberates religion from formalism and ritual, and in opening the church to all mankind, Greeks as well as Jews, women as well as men, slaves as well as freemen, strikes to the true basis of democracy.

I CORINTHIANS

Paul's next westward journey (usually called his Third Missionary Journey) took him to Ephesus, for a long stay of more than two years, and there he was in somewhat frequent communication with his Christian friends at Corinth, just across the Ægean Sea. So began the most extended correspondence of Paul's that we know of, for eventually he wrote the Corinthians at least four letters, one referred to in I Corinthians, 5:9, and so evidently preceding our I Corinthians; a second, known to us as I Corinthians; a third, that must have preceded our II Corinthians, but not identical with our I Corinthians; and finally II Corinthians, or at least chs. 1 to 9 of it, since chs. 10 to 13 may be the missing third letter.

Paul's first letter to them, which he mentions in I Corinthians 5:9—"I wrote you in my letter"—is lost; unless it is preserved in part in a passage on the subject, in II Cor. 6:14 to 7:1, which seems to have no connection with its context. Read it, as a possible part of the lost letter, which warned the Corinthians "not to associate with immoral people."

While Paul was absorbed in preaching the gospel to the Ephesians, visitors from Corinth told him of factions and evils in the life of the church there, and then a delegation from Corinth arrived with a letter full of practical problems in their church life. Paul's answer to this letter is what we know as I Corinthians.

Read Paul's correction of the faults of which he had learned from the first group of visitors from Corinth, chs. 1 to 6. Then read chs. 7 to 15, in which he takes up the questions raised by the letter from Corinth: marriage, and the relations of the sexes, ch. 7; whether they should continue to buy their meat at the temple markets, chs. 8 to 10; behavior in church, chs. 11 to 14, especially how women should dress, and how the Lord's Supper should be observed, ch. 11; and then what should be done about ecstatic speaking, which was breaking up their meetings, chs. 12 to 14. In ch. 15 Paul deals with the resurrection hope. The closing chapter deals with business and personal matters.

Such was the question box the Corinthians had sent Paul. Some of their questions were on somewhat insignificant matters, but Paul takes them all very seriously. In his answers, he shows himself a great teacher and thinker, taking their problems up patiently and working them through with the Corinthians to some great principle of action, of far wider application and valid still, like the ninth chapter, in which

Paul shows that there is sometimes a better use of one's rights than to insist upon them, or the thirteenth chapter, on love and its supreme place in Christian living. Here Paul discovers Christian courtesy, which has done so much to adorn life.

II CORINTHIANS

What Paul had said in I Corinthians about the factions at Corinth evidently stung the Corinthians and alienated them from Paul, and this led him to write them another letter, vigorously defending himself against the attacks being made upon him at Corinth. The last four chapters of II Corinthians probably belong to that letter, for they reflect a different stage of the controversy from that dealt with in chs. 1 to 9, where all is peace and harmony again. It would seem that chs. 10 to 13 make up the letter written at the height of the conflict, and referred to in II Cor. 2:3, 4 and 7:8, 9. Certainly in 2:4 Paul almost apologizes for having written as he had done, an attitude he could not possibly have taken with reference to I Corinthians. Read II Cor., chs. 10 to 13, then, as the third letter in Paul's correspondence with Corinth, and note the fiery indignation Paul shows at the way in which the Corinthians have gone back on him. He cannot have said all these harsh things about them in the same letter in which he approves of them so unreservedly as he does in chs. 1 to 9, especially in 7:11–16.

In chs. 1 to 9, however, we are in an atmosphere of complete reconciliation. All misunderstandings are past, and Paul can say, "At every point you have proved that you are clear of this matter," 7:11. They are now as zealous in support of

Paul as they had been hostile before. Paul meets this new mood with a resurvey of their differences in gentler mood, and the result is a statement of the motives and methods of his ministry, 2:12 to 6:10. This is of great interest and importance, not only for the light it throws upon missionary work in the very first stages of the Christian mission, but as a self-portrait of the Apostle Paul himself. It was by such means and methods that he carried the gospel so far and so fast over the Greek world. "Not that we are the masters of you and your faith; we are working with you to make you happy," 1:24. "It is by the open statement of the truth that I would commend myself to every human conscience in the sight of God," 4:2. "For it is not myself but Christ Jesus that I am proclaiming as Lord; I am only a slave of yours for Jesus' sake," 4:5. Chapters 8 and 9, concerned with business and the collection for the Jerusalem poor, seem to form the conclusion of the letter.

If as we have seen, I Corinthians takes the roof off the Corinthians' meeting place and lets us look inside, II Corinthians gives us an even more intimate picture, for it actually lets us look into the heart of Paul.

Read chs. 1 to 9, therefore, as the last letter in Paul's correspondence with Corinth, which may be outlined as follows:

1. The letter spoken of in I Cor. 5:9, to which the detached fragment in II Cor. 6:14 to 7:1 probably belongs.

2. I Corinthians, written at Ephesus, in A.D. 54, in reply to a letter from the Corinthians, I Cor. 7:1.

3. The harsh, painful letter, written at Ephesus in A.D. 55, in great distress, with many tears, carried by Titus, and regretted after it was sent, probably our II Cor., chs. 10 to 13.

4. The letter of reconciliation, sent from Macedonia in A.D. 55, preserved in II Cor., chs. 1 to 9.

ROMANS

Soon after Paul had sent his great letter of reconciliation to the Corinthians, II Cor., chs. 1 to 9, from Macedonia, he followed it to Corinth, probably hoping that he might go on from Corinth to Rome, and lay a guiding hand upon the church already established in that strategic city. But the collection for the poor of Jerusalem which he had been organizing among his churches was now completed and must be taken to Jerusalem by someone who understood its motive and could interpret it properly to the Christians there. Paul's plan of visiting Rome, and going on to Spain to spread the gospel there must be postponed. So, as he cannot go in person, Paul puts what he considers the heart of the gospel into a letter and sends it on to Rome, while he turns his face eastward for Jerusalem.

In this letter, which we know as Romans, Paul explains the place in the Christian life, of faith—that experience in the human heart of the presence, the forgiveness, and the love of God. For the gospel's good news was not that God had condemned the world; he had forgiven the world, and all that man has to do is to adopt the attitude of faith and accept that forgiveness. If he does, he will be freed from the Law and follow the guidance of the spirit of God in his heart.

Greeks and Jews, Paul sees, have all failed to achieve true uprightness, chs. 1; 2. But through Christ a way to attain it has now been revealed; the way of faith, that is, a spirit of trust, obedience, and sonship to God, ch. 3. Paul illustrates this from the stories of Abraham and Adam, chs. 4 and 5. Those who adopt this attitude of faith and accept the forgiveness God freely offers escape from the dominion of sin and law, and enter upon a new life, chs. 6 to 8.

This is the main argument of Romans. Read these eight chapters with this simple outline in mind.

One of the great objections Greeks had to offer to the Christian missionary was the fact that so few Jews had accepted Christ as their Messiah. Paul has an answer to this objection, chs. 9 to 11, which form an appendix to the body of the letter to the Romans. He usually concluded his letters with a few moral admonitions, but in Romans these build up into the greatest statement of Christian behavior in the New Testament, except the Sermon on the Mount, 12:1 to 15:13. Chapter 14, for example, is a great appeal for Christian tolerance, as much needed now as when Paul wrote it. The rest of ch. 15 tells of Paul's plans and movements. The sixteenth chapter is a letter of introduction for a Christian woman named Phoebe who is setting out from Cenchreæ, the Ægean port of Corinth, apparently for Rome, and Paul wishes to make her known to a number of Christians who will entertain her and further her plans. This letter is an interesting glimpse of the operation of Christian hospitality, so necessary for travelers in the corrupt ancient world.

Read the second half of Romans with this analysis in mind, observing Paul's hopes for the salvation of the Jews, in chs. 9 to 11, his standard of Christian morals, 12:1 to 15:13, his affairs and plans, 15:14–33, and his Christian helpfulness, ch. 16. And consider the breadth of his interests, as he turns eastward with the collection in a vain effort to reconcile the Jewish wing of the church to the Greek one, but sends this great letter westward to help in shaping Christianity in the capital of the ancient world.

PHILIPPIANS

Christ's example of humility and obedience to his Father's will has always been an inspiration to Christian living and the pursuit of the Christian ideal; and Christian faith has seen that in the most adverse circumstances we can still guide our thoughts to wholesome and lofty things.

These are some of the lessons of Philippians.

It was while a prisoner in Rome that Paul pointed these things out in his unforgettable manner to his friends in Philippi. His plans for a missionary journey to Spain had been thwarted by his arrest in Jerusalem and his imprisonment, first in Cæsarea and then in Rome. But in Rome he was cheered by the help of his old friends, the Christians of Philippi, who raised a sum of money for his use and sent one of their number named Epaphroditus on to Rome to do anything that could be done for him. In acknowledging their gifts Paul disclosed some of the deepest aspects of his religious experience.

Philippians seems to consist of two letters from Paul to the Philippians, one beginning with an impassioned warning against the Judaizers and going on to acknowledge the arrival of Epaphroditus with their gift, 3:2 to 4:23; and the other telling them of the progress of the gospel in other lands, calling upon them to meet persecution in the spirit of Christ, and explaining the return of Epaphroditus to Philippi in consequence of his illness in Rome, 1:1 to 3:1.

Read Philippians in this order, beginning with 3:2 to

4:23, the letter of acknowledgment; and going on with 1:1 to
3:1, the letter carried back to Philippi by Epaphroditus on
his return there—for its picture of practical helpfulness in
the Early Church, its understanding of the spirit of Christ,
and its high ideals of Christian living, even in the most dis-
couraging situations and conditions.

COLOSSIANS

   The Christian finds in Christ the all-sufficient intermediary
between the soul and God, and no formal observance of fasts
and vigils is necessary to attain the full religious experience
of the presence of God and of communion with him, to which
Christ introduces the believer. In the Christian fellowship,
moreover, there can be no higher inner circles; the fullest
attainment is open to all alike.

   These Christian truths Paul set forth in a letter to the
Christian brethren in Colossæ, in the heart of western Asia
Minor, where other ideas of Christ's place in religion were
being proclaimed. Some converts there had brought with them
the Greek idea of rising through communion with range after
range of intermediate beings or ideas into the full experience
of God, and thought of Christ as just one of these intermediaries.

   News of this had been carried to Paul, in his prison in
Rome, by Epaphras, the minister of the church at Colossæ,
and led Paul to set forth Christ's supreme place in religion;
these other supposed intermediaries were mere delusions.
With them he dismissed such formal practices as fasts and
vigils, and the claims of a higher spirituality made by those
who practiced them. All that Christ has to give, he pointed

out, is open to every believer: "In spreading the news of him, we warn everyone and teach everyone all our wisdom, in order to bring everyone to Christian perfection." This is Christianity's great democratic ideal.

Read Col. 1:1 to 2:23, in which Paul disposes of the views and practices that are invading the Colossian church; then 2:24 to 4:6, with its practical injunctions, especially for wives and husbands, children and fathers, and slaves and masters. Tychicus is to carry the letter to Colossæ, and to take Onesimus with him. A number of Paul's friends and lieutenants are with Paul, perhaps because his case is reaching its crisis, 4:7–18.

PHILEMON

The last lines of Colossians refer them to another letter Paul is sending to the neighboring church at Laodicea, eleven miles away. In fact, he wishes these two churches to exchange letters, Laodicea reading Colossians and Colossæ reading Laodiceans. In Colossians he also tells the Colossians to take a message for him to Archippus, who is mentioned as if he were not at Colossæ but at Laodicea. What has become of the letter to the Laodiceans?

The little letter to Philemon is the answer.

For it is not merely a letter to Philemon but to our sister Apphia and our fellow-soldier Archippus, and the church that meets in Philemon's house. Here is Archippus, whom we expect from Col. 4:16, 17 to find in Laodicea. There is every reason to suppose that a letter so definitely mentioned as Laodiceans is in Colossians would not be lost; both letters would probably be preserved in both churches. It would take some such support to preserve so small a note as Philemon, only a page long, until it found a place in a collection of Paul's letters, about thirty years later.

The situation is very simple. Philemon's slave Onesimus had run away and found his way to Rome, where he had fallen under Christian influences and met Paul. Paul learns his story and decides to send him back to his master in Colossæ. This exposed him to any kind of punishment his master might order; it might even cost him his life. Paul is taking a great risk with Onesimus. But he does all he can to protect him. He writes a letter to Philemon, asking him to welcome the runaway as a Christian brother. He sends this not only to Philemon but to his wife, as we suppose, his minister Archippus, Paul's "fellow-soldier," and the church that meets in Philemon's house. The fate of Onesimus is to be settled in the presence of the Laodicean church. Not only that, but Colossæ and Laodicea are to exchange letters, so that the Colossian church too will know what Philemon decides to do. Paul puts his whole influence back of the runaway slave he is sending home to his master, and calls upon him to receive the runaway with true Christian forgiveness.

EPHESIANS

There is no nobler view of the Christian Church than that which conceives it as a great world-wide spiritual fellowship of all those who through the mercy of God have entered upon the new life. This is especially developed in the letter to the Ephesians, which also appealed to second-generation

Christianity to realize the supreme worth of their religion, especially as it was revealed in the letters of Paul. The letter begins with a tumultuous rhapsody on the blessings of the Christian salvation, and goes on to set forth its inestimable worth. It was evidently written by a later follower of Paul, perhaps the collector of his letters, to form the introduction to the collected letters of Paul when toward the end of the first century, soon after the appearance of Luke and The Acts, they were gathered up and published.

Read Ephesians as an introduction to Paul's collected letters, addressed to Christians everywhere, since, unlike Paul's own letters, it was intended for publication. It was a time when second-generation Christians, threatened with the apathy that familiarity so often brings, needed to be reminded of the surpassing worth of their faith. After a jubilant summary of the blessings of salvation, 1:3–14, the supreme value of the Christian faith is set forth, 1:15–23. By the mercy of God, the believer enters on a new life, 2:1–10, which is open to Greek as well as Jew, 2:11–22. Paul in his letters, which they should read, has declared that the heathen have equal rights with the Jews in the new religion, 3:1–13, which opens to them a great experience of Christ's love, 3:14–21. Believers must be united against the sects just beginning to appear, 4:1–16, and live the new Christian life, 4:17 to 6:24.

Ephesians marks the transition from the personal letter, addressing a single group of believers, to the epistle, a general or encyclical letter, meant for Christians everywhere. Most of the remaining letters in the New Testament are epistles, written for the widest possible public.

HEBREWS

A generation after Paul had written his great letter to the church at Rome another Christian teacher wrote that church a letter, which we know as Hebrews. Christianity in Rome was in its second generation, and, as so often happens, people who had grown up in a Christian circle had lost their sense of its worth. Apathy was threatening the Roman church.

It had a great past; thirty years before it had stood up heroically before Nero's persecution, and now Domitian's demand of emperor worship as a test of loyalty from his very miscellaneous subjects all around the Mediterranean again threatened them with the old peril of apostasy. Would they give up their Christian faith and obey the emperor's new demand?

To remind them of the immense value of that faith and the fearful consequences of disowning it, Hebrews was written. It compares Christianity with the next greatest religion they knew of, Judaism, and shows how point by point the new religion vastly excels the old. Read Hebrews from this point of view, as it shows how much greater Christ was than the revealers of Judaism were; how he was prepared for his high priesthood by a great experience of suffering; how far he was above Moses and the old high priests; how much better the sacrifice that he offered, for it was himself. All this is interspersed with impassioned warnings against giving up such a religion.

In a splendid passage, ch. 11, the writer tells of the great heroes of Judaism, who had not seen the fulfilment of their hopes, but had died in faith, without having received what had been promised them. The Roman Christians must follow their great example, and accept the discipline of life. Then, in a final comparison, the writer points out the superiority of the Christian faith and the dreadful consequences of forsaking it.

Hebrews is rhetorically the most eloquent book in the New Testament. It does not hesitate to resort to allegory in its argument, and its picture of Judaism is drawn from the Old Testament, not from contemporary Jewish life, for Jerusalem had long since fallen and the high priests no longer functioned in the Temple. The writer has put his message in the form of a letter, but it reads more like a great oration and, of course, it was intended to be read aloud to a meeting of the church at Rome.

I PETER

The modern Christian naturally intends to be a good citizen of his country, but the early Christians lived under a pagan government which did not regard their religion as legal, and sometimes attacked them. The demand for emperor worship as a token of loyalty to the empire was one Christians could not possibly comply with, and threatened to drive them into disloyalty and sedition. But a nobler solution of the problem was proposed in I Peter, which called on the Christian brotherhood to obey the state, respect the emperor, and love even their enemies. This was the true attitude for the church to assume in the face of persecution.

Hebrews had just called upon the church at Rome to teach the churches, Heb. 5:12, and in I Peter that church responded to its demand. It felt that it could speak in the name of Peter since he had suffered martyrdom in Rome, and the Roman church was the custodian of his tomb and teaching. So in his name, the church of Rome writes to the churches of Asia Minor to take this higher and harder view of persecution.

Read I Peter for a touching picture of the Christian's duties in the world, the state, and the church, as they appeared to the leaders of the Roman church about A.D. 95. If persecution came, it must be endured as part of the will of God; "Therefore those who suffer by the will of God must intrust their souls to a Creator who is faithful, and continue to do what is right."

This was the patient heroism which was later to overcome the world.

JAMES

The sermon or homily that we know as the Epistle of James was probably written about the end of the first century or early in the second, but not as an epistle. It really belongs among the orations, where we have already discussed it. It was later made to serve as an epistle by being published to the whole Christian brotherhood.

I, II, AND III JOHN

True Christianity has always meant a great spiritual experience of the love of God as shown in Christ, finding expression in uprightness, goodness, and obedience. The Christian belongs to a great spiritual fellowship in which the bond is love.

This great idea was set forth with the greatest simplicity and force, early in the second century, in the letters of John. They were written to be carried by missionaries going out from Ephesus, through the province of Asia. III John is addressed to a Christian named Gaius, while II John is written to the church to which Gaius belonged. But they are little more than covering letters for I John, which is for all the churches the missionary may reach, and carries the message of this great spiritual fellowship. Its great lesson is that as children of God we must love one another, for God is Love.

The writer does not give his name; he is simply "The Elder," and as such is evidently so well known throughout Asia that any church would know at once who he was. He was naturally identified with John the famous elder, or presbyter, of Ephesus, and so these letters have come down to us under the name of John.

Read III John, the personal letter, first; then II John, the letter to the church of which Gaius was a member; and finally, I John, which carries the great lesson which has been called "Fellowship in the Life Eternal."

JUDE

Among the sects that made their appearance in Christian circles early in the second century was Docetism, which held that only Christ's material body suffered on the cross, his divine nature having escaped it. Such thinkers found little religious meaning in his death, but they thought themselves so good that they needed no atonement. They were so confident of this that they attached no importance to their bodily natures, giving free reign to their passions while priding themselves upon their spiritual attainments.

Sometime between A.D. 125 and 150 a Christian leader named Jude sent out among the churches a little tract written with great vigor denouncing such teachings and doings, and warning Christians everywhere against being misled by them. His missive is a brief but terrible invective, rich in Old Testament allusions and reflecting also later Jewish books, such as the Book of Enoch and the Assumption of Moses, vs. 6, 9, and 14, but most powerful in its own fearful arraignment of these schismatics, whose pretensions and self-indulgence made them a serious menace to the life of the churches.

Read the Epistle of Jude for a glimpse of the grave dangers that threatened the Christian movement toward the middle of the second century.

I AND II TIMOTHY, AND TITUS

As Christian groups grew larger and their work became more varied, the need for more definite organization of each local church came to be felt. Every church had to handle money, and there must be responsible men to do this. All the church officers must be tried and faithful people, for the church was under constant observation, and any laxity would bring discredit upon its work. The various groups in the church must be shown their particular responsibilities and duties.

It was to effect this that about the middle of the second century the letters to Timothy and Titus were written, in the name of Paul, the great founder of Greek Christianity, and as an appendix to his published letters. They are addressed to his famous lieutenants Timothy and Titus, as representing Christian missionaries and pastors generally, telling them how to organize the churches and conduct their work.

Read I Timothy, then Titus, then II Timothy (for that is evidently the order in which they are intended to be understood, as Paul is again in prison in II Timothy), for their picture of the Early Church organizing for more efficient work. Note the frequent warnings against the sects, which were in full swing in A.D. 150; the authorization of a twofold ministry, overseers (or presbyters), and deacons; and the definite adoption of the Old Testament as the book of the church, II Tim. 3:16, against the sect of Marcion, which rejected it.

II PETER

The last book of the New Testament to be written was II Peter. It was concerned with the vexed matter of the return of Christ to the world in a Second Coming, a doctrine advanced by Paul in more than one of his letters, but spiritualized in John as the coming of the Holy Spirit into the believer's heart. II Peter vigorously defends the earlier view, and appropriates almost all of Jude's invective against the Docetists, directing it now against those who deny the Second Coming. He seems to have particularly in mind the second-century sect known as the Marcosians, for the vices with which he charges them were characteristic of that group— immoral and mercenary conduct, doctrinal vagaries, magic, and allegory.

Although the writer assumes the rôle of Peter, not only

in the address, 1:1, but here and there through the epistle,
1:14–18; 3:1; he shows acquaintance with the collection of
the Four Gospels, the collected letters of Paul, 3:15,
Hebrews, I Peter, and Jude. Indeed, he speaks of Paul's
letters as Scripture, 3:16, and as being twisted to their own
purposes by some sect, evidently the Marcionites, who appeared toward the middle of the second century.

Read II Peter not only for its stern picture of the perils
that threatened both the thought and the character of the
church in the second century, but for the fine Christian ideal
set forth in the opening paragraph, with its chain of Christian
virtues beginning with faith and ending with love, 1:5–9.

CHAPTER NINETEEN

Visions and Revelations

NOT A few of the Hebrew prophets experienced times of ecstasy, when in visions they felt themselves in the very presence of God, heard him speak, and saw celestial realities. Sometimes they saw in the natural scenes about them deeper meanings of great religious importance. And sometimes they used visions as literary vehicles for their messages to their people. In these ways great religious lessons of moral instruction and direction, and of hope and encouragement in times of persecution and danger were conveyed to their hearers. It was the hope of the Prophet Joel that a day would come when the Spirit of God would pervade all kinds of people, young and old, male and female, slave and free, when the old men would dream dreams and the young men see visions, Joel 2:28, 29. The greatest of the prophets sometimes found their way to truth through visions.

Amos, the first of the literary prophets, often fell into such ecstatic states. God showed him the plague of locusts threatening the land, and then the fire. Then he saw the Lord with the plumb line in his hand, 7:1–9. Then came the vision of the basket of summer fruit, and of the Lord standing beside the altar, 9:1–4.

Once when Isaiah was in the Temple, he had a great

vision of God upon his throne, heard the angels chanting "Holy, holy, holy!" and received his call to preach. It was the year that King Uzziah died, 740 B.C. (Isa., ch. 6.)

Jeremiah's call, too, came to him in a vision, 1:4–19, when the Lord touched his mouth, and said:

> "See! I put my words in your mouth;
>   This day I give you authority over the nations and kingdoms,
>   To root up and to pull down, to wreck and to ruin,
>   To build and to plant." (Jer. 1:9, 10.)

Other visions of Jeremiah's are the almond tree, 1:11, 12; the boiling pot, 1:13–19, the two baskets of figs, 24:1–10, and the wine cup of wrath, 25:15–29.

EZEKIEL

Ezekiel's visions are an even more characteristic feature of his prophetic work; about one-fourth of his book consists of visions. His call came to him in his great vision of the Glory of God, usually spoken of as the Vision of Ezekiel, 1:1 to 3:15. The visions of the idolatry in the Temple culminate in the solemn departure of the glory of God from Jerusalem, chs. 8 to 11. Perhaps the greatest of them was the vision of the Valley of the Dry Bones, 37:1–14. Ezekiel's great plan for the new Temple, chs. 40 to 42, together with the regulations to govern its worship, is described as a vision, chs. 40 to 46, including the future return of God's glory to Jerusalem, 43:1–4. The last vision in the book is that of the refreshing perennial stream that shall flow from the future temple, 47:1–12. Visions played a greater part in the work of Ezekiel than in that of any previous prophet.

Read these visions of Ezekiel as meant by the prophet to rouse his depressed and bewildered companions, transferred from their own land to a foreign heathen country, to a sense of the enduring value of their people and their faith, and to prepare them for the distant day when they might return to their own soil and resume their worship of God in a better temple than the one they had seen destroyed. His emphasis upon the religious as distinguished from the national future of the Jews has led to his being called the father of Judaism, and in the meeting of the elders in his house to hear him speak, we can see the beginnings of the Jewish synagogue.

ZECHARIAH

When Haggai was urging the rebuilding of the Temple in Jerusalem, in 520 B.C., he was seconded in his efforts by the Prophet Zechariah. It was two months after Haggai's first sermon that Zechariah began to speak, and he continued to do so after Haggai's last sermon, two months later. So his work began before the end of 520 B.C. and continued into 519. The first eight chapters of Zechariah which preserve his preaching are almost entirely visions. The vision of the Horseman Among the Myrtle Trees and the Heavenly Patrol, with its promise of restoration, the vision of the Four Horns and their destroyers, of the Man with the Measuring Line, the Lamp and the Olive Trees, the flying roll and the woman in the measure, and finally the Four Chariots make up the bulk of Zechariah's sermons as we know them. They taught in symbol the purification of the land and its protection, and awakened fresh hopes for the future greatness of Jerusalem. It would be so large that no wall could enclose it. Old men and women

would again be seen in the city, and the streets would be full
of playing children. A great religious destiny still awaited
Israel: "In those days, ten men, from nations of every
language, shall lay hold of him who is a Jew, saying, 'Let
us go with you; for we have heard that God is with you!'"
(Zech. 8:23.) Later prophecies from other hands, chs. 9 to
14, enlarge upon Zechariah's bright hopes for Israel's future.
They form a little apocalyptic drama, probably from the third
century before Christ. The city will be holy; even the bells on
the horses' harness will bear the words, "Holy to the Lord"
(14:20). And some day, the Messiah himself will come:

> "Humble, and riding upon an ass,
>   Even upon a colt, the foal of an ass. . . .
>   And he shall command peace upon the nations." (Zech. 9:9, 10.)

DANIEL

In the bitter struggle of the pious Jews against their
Syrian rulers who were trying to make them give up their
Law and adopt Greek civilization, 168–165 B.C., they took
courage from heroic stories of the persecutions of older times,
when in the Exile in Babylonia the Jews had to stand out
against a triumphant idolatry. These took shape in The Book
of Daniel, the first half of which, chs. 1 to 6, consists of six
stories of Hebrew heroism in captivity in Babylon. The second
half, chs. 7 to 12, describes four visions, and constitutes the
flower of Old Testament apocalyptic.

The Jews had come to think that with Ezra the age of
inspiration had ended, for it was then that the Law had
reached its full and final form and been solemnly accepted

by the Jews of Jerusalem, as related in Neh., chs. 8 to 10. So if a Jew of later time felt he had a divine communication to give his people, he set it forth as the work of some ancient, long before Ezra, and described it as meant "not for this generation, but for a remote one which is to come," as The Book of Enoch so well expressed it, Enoch 1:2. This is the meaning of Dan. 8:26: "Keep the vision a secret, for it relates to the distant future," and of 12:9: "The words are bound up and sealed till the time of the end." So the ecstatic visions of the older prophets gave way to a literary device by which a later prophet gave his message the name of some antique figure, Enoch, Noah, Daniel, or Ezra, intended not for their times but for the time of its actual author, the theory being that it had been kept secret until the time for which it was intended.

Daniel was one of the traditional Hebrew heroes, classed by Ezekiel with Noah and Job, Ezek. 14:14, and in the soul-trying days of the Maccabæan struggle, which began in 168 B.C., he became the symbol and pattern of Jewish loyalty and courage, as told in Dan., chs. 1 to 6. Then follows the apocalyptic part of the book, chs. 7 to 12, in four visions.

The first is the vision of the Four Beasts rising from the sea, to symbolize four empires, beginning with Babylon. From the fourth, the Greek empire founded by Alexander in 334 B.C., a king shall arise who

"shall plan to change the sacred seasons and the law,
And they shall be handed over to him for a year, two years, and half a year.
Then . . . the kingdom . . . shall be given to the people of the saints of the Most High;
Their kingdom shall be an everlasting kingdom,
And all dominions shall serve and obey them." (Dan. 7:25, 27.)

The three years and a half were the time of the Maccabæan conflict, 168–165 B.C., from the beginning of Antiochus' persecution to the rededication of the Temple by the Pious party led by Judas Maccabæus—the "saints," as they came to be called. In the being who appeared on the clouds of heaven and was promised that all people should serve him and his dominion should not pass away, 7:13, 14, The Book of Enoch a century later recognized the Messiah.

The second vision was that of the Ram and the He-goat, ch. 8, which is explained in some detail. The He-goat's great horn is Alexander the Great; the four horns that took its place were the four kingdoms of his successors, and the little horn is evidently Antiochus Epiphanes, whose determined policy of Hellenizing the Jews led to the Maccabæan uprising in 168 B.C.

The third vision, of the Seventy Weeks, ch. 9, explains that Jeremiah's prophecy that the Babylonian captivity should last seventy years, Jer. 25:12; 29:10, really meant seventy weeks of years, or 490 years. Counting from the final fall of Jerusalem in 586 B.C., he makes this period reach its conclusion in the year 165 B.C. when the "Pious" Jews led by Judas Maccabæus dislodged the Syrians from Jerusalem and reëstablished their Temple worship. This makes Jeremiah's prophecies refer to the success of the Maccabæan struggle, although as a matter of fact, seventy weeks of years would carry us not to 165 but to 96 B.C. But the final "week" in which many abandon the covenant, and the half "week" for which the sacrifice and offering cease, seem clearly to mean the seven years of Antiochus' campaign against Judaism, for the last three years of which the Temple worship was displaced by heathen rites.

On the whole, the highly fanciful expansion of Jeremiah's predicted duration of the Exile, the round number of seventy years, to seven times that length of time, seems to reveal the writer's consciousness that in a sense the Exile had lasted till his own day and was only just ending. For, although the Jews were indeed released by Cyrus in 538 B.C. and allowed to return home, they were not yet free, but still subjects of Persia, and subjects they remained of Persia, Greece, or Syria, for centuries, until the "exile," thought of as national subjection, had lasted well-nigh seven times the seventy years of Jeremiah's prediction. But now their Syrian masters have been defeated and driven from Jerusalem, and while the Jews were not yet really independent, independence for the first time in more than four hundred years began to appear possible. Then indeed the "exile" would be over. It is true, this concern for political freedom did not long interest the Pharisees, but it certainly stirred the author of Daniel to offer his bold revision of Jeremiah's prophecy.

The Exile proper lasted at the longest barely sixty years, from 597 to 538 B.C., and seven times its actual duration would bring one very near the year of the Maccabæan triumph, 165 B.C., if one reckoned from the death of Zedekiah, the last king of Judah, as Daniel does. And an apocalyptic writer could easily reckon in both ways at the same time.

The fourth vision, chs. 10 to 12, the Conflict of the Kingdoms, reviews the history from Cyrus the Great, 538 B.C., down to the death of Antiochus Epiphanes, the persecuting king of Syria, in 164 B.C., to be attended by the deliverance of the Jewish people, blended with hopes of resurrection for the just. It is strange that the writer mentions only four kings of Persia, out of at least ten known to history between 538 and 333 B.C., probably knowing only the four mentioned in the Old Testament, Cyrus, Xerxes, Artaxerxes I, and Darius III. His knowledge of the Babylonian monarchs was equally meager, for he made Belshazzar the son of Nebuchadnezzar, instead of Nabonidus, ch. 5, and credited the taking of Babylon to Darius instead of Cyrus, Dan. 5:31. But about the history from Alexander down, that is, after 333 B.C., the wars and intermarriages of the Ptolemies in Egypt and the Seleucidae in Syria, he is much better informed, although he narrates them in the obscure, cryptic fashion usual in apocalyptic literature. The vision ends with the angel's assurance that the persecution will last three and a half years, 12:7, though somewhat longer periods are indicated in the numbers given in vs. 11 and 12.

Daniel introduces us to the figures of the archangels Gabriel and Michael, and to the Pharisaic doctrine of resurrection, not like the Christian one, a general resurrection, a way of expressing immortality, but the rising of a select few, very good or very bad, 12:2, 3. Its art was the art of the grotesque, and its symbolic style confined the understanding of it to the initiated, the Pious party, who had the key to its symbolism.

Read The Book of Daniel as the beginning of a new type of Jewish literature, the Apocalypse, or Revelation, written between 168 and 164 B.C. to sustain and stimulate hopes of success in the breasts of the ragged, desperate band of Jewish volunteers who followed Judas Maccabæus through his daring uphill fight for the preservation of the Jewish faith; chs. 1 to 6, for stirring tales of Jewish heroism in the days of the Exile, and chs. 7 to 12 for visions of final success and the dawn of a better day.

II ESDRAS

The Second Book of Esdras, as it has been called since the Geneva Bible of 1560, is so confused and perplexing that Luther said he threw it into the Elbe. It stands second among the Apocrypha in the King James Version, as it had always stood in English Bibles. It is no wonder it bewildered and annoyed Luther, for it possesses all the intentional obscurity characteristic of any single apocalypse and more too, for it is a collection of such revelations, dating all the way from the outbreak of the Jewish War in A.D. 66 to the years following the Decian persecution, probably A.D. 260–270. So the situations reflected in the various parts of the book are scattered over two hundred years, until finally a Greek Christian impressed by the apparent collapse of Roman authority in the east, toward A.D. 270, took a group of Jewish apocalypses, gave them an earlier Christian preface, chs. 1 and 2, written about A.D. 150, and completed the collection with a conclusion of his own, chs. 15 and 16.

The body of the book consists of the so-called Ezra apocalypse, chs. 3 to 10, written probably in Hebrew about A.D. 100. It contains four visions, in which Ezra asks God some questions relating to his dealings with his people Israel.

To this work three further visions have been added. The fifth, the Eagle Vision, written in Domitian's time, A.D. 81–96, portrays the conflict between the empire and the Messiah. The sixth, the Man from the Sea, was written about the time the Jewish War broke out, A.D. 66. A man rises from the sea and gathers the ten tribes, which had been hidden somewhere in the mountains of the east. The Man is the preëxistent

Messiah, the Son of God, and the vision is decidedly Christian in color. The seventh is the Writing of the Books, and clearly seeks to relate Ezra with the completion of the Hebrew Scriptures. It was probably written early in the second century after Christ.

Altogether, II Esdras is full of interest for Jewish and Christian thought and hope through the two hundred years which gradually produced it. Its earliest portion, the sixth vision, of the Man from the Sea, is older than the Revelation of John, but the book took on its final form and reached completion a full century after the last book in the New Testament was written.

Read II Esdras for its pictures of the hopes in which Jew and Christian found cheer in times of persecution through the two tempestuous centuries that followed the outbreak of the Jewish War with Rome, in A.D. 66; the varied questions that troubled the Jewish mind, and the wide variety of apocalyptic expression assembled into this single book.

THE REVELATION OF JOHN

In our troubled times many religious people turn to the book of Revelation, with all its calamities and woes, for light upon what is happening and going to happen, and its hideous pictures of disaster and distress have never been more dreadfully realized than now. Its apocalyptic vocabulary of monsters and marvels seems peculiarly appropriate to what has been going on all over the world in our own day, and it may well claim our serious attention.

It was written in a time when the forces of righteousness and faith seemed threatened with extinction. The Roman

Empire's demand of emperor worship as a token of loyalty from all its subjects except the Jews, brought it for the first time into collision with the young Christian Church, and threatened the church with immediate destruction. But the Christian prophet declares that whatever disasters may overtake the world and threaten the church, the one certain thing about the future is the final triumph of the Kingdom of God. So the Christian is to move undismayed through plague, famine, war, invasion, earthquake, flood, and death, sure that the sovereignty of the world will finally belong to our God and his Christ, and he will reign forever and ever.

The demand by Domitian of emperor worship as a test of loyalty to the Roman Empire (about A.D. 90) was one which Christian believers could not possibly meet. Christians had always been in a precarious position, for their religion had never been recognized as permitted or licensed by the empire. But this new demand put them in an impossible position and made their prospects dark indeed. How could they hope to resist the Roman Empire, the greatest political and military force in their world? The great temptation was to compromise; to go through the simple little ceremony of burning a pinch of incense before the emperor's statue, bowing before it, and uttering the affirmation, Cæsar is a god. So easily could the personal peril be averted and the church itself preserved, for if all the Christians refused the demand they would all perish and the church with them.

In this fearful situation, John, a prophet of Ephesus, resorted to apocalyptic. He had no need to write in the name of some famous ancient Hebrew, for the Christians believed that the spirit of God was again speaking to his people, so he wrote in his own name, speaking boldly as a prophet who was in exile for his faith, on the rocky island of Patmos, off the coast of Asia. He writes to his own church at Ephesus and the leading churches of the province of Asia, calling upon them to stand firm against the demands being made upon them. His book is to be read in public in the churches, for he pronounces a blessing upon the man who reads it and upon those who hear it read, 1:3. He writes in the cryptic language of apocalyptic, which made his book a code message to those familiar with the vocabulary and imagery of such visions, while it would remain meaningless to the uninitiated Roman official who might chance to read it. But to its Christian readers it offered a great moral reinforcement of indomitable hope in the final triumph of their cause.

Strangely enough, although the book is an apocalypse, or revelation, in the tradition of Daniel and of The Book of Enoch (first century before Christ) what we may call the portal of The Revelation of John is formed by a group of eight letters, a general one to the seven churches of the Roman province of Asia—Ephesus, Smyrna, Pergamum, Thyatira, Sardis, Philadelphia, and Laodicea—followed by short messages hardly two hundred words long to each of the seven, calling upon them to withstand the persecution that was threatening them, evidently in the latter days of Domitian, A.D. 90–96.

It is clear, however, that the letters are not sent singly, but all together, as a group, accompanied by the general letter to all seven, ch. 1. Each church is to read all the letters. Indeed, they are evidently written as a part of the Revelation, and included in its publication, for the warning against any alteration of the book in its transmission, 22:18, 19, shows that John expects it to be copied and circulated. It is impossible to think such a collection of letters, to Christian churches, seven in number, prefaced with a general letter to all seven, was not influenced by the recent appearance of just such a collection of Paul's personal letters, to Christian churches, seven in number, accompanied by a general letter to Christians everywhere. Revelation is, in fact, the first book to show the influence of the collected and published letters of Paul.

Following this group of letters, which serve as introduction to the book, the main body of Revelation consists of three great visions, 4:1 to 22:5.

They are cast in the grotesque imagery and mysterious vocabulary of the old apocalyptic, as it was found in Dan., chs. 7 to 12, which would hide the prophet's meaning from ordinary eyes but awaken the interest and stimulate the attention of Christians familiar with Daniel, Enoch, and other apocalyptic books. But the influence of contemporary Greek drama is also to be seen in the Revelation, for it has its arias and antiphonies, its choruses of saints and elders, 4:4, 10; 14:3, and its prodigious orchestration, for its accompaniments are not only harps and trumpets, 5:8; 14:2; chs. 8; 9, but earthquakes, thunders, and the noise of mighty waters. So the Revelation is not simply another example of Jewish apocalyptic, but shows the influence also of Paul's collected letters and of contemporary Greek drama as well.

We must approach the Revelation therefore as a mighty super-opera, with three great acts, each broken into scenes of agony or beauty, and with mighty choruses and terrific bursts of the cosmic orchestra punctuating its action.

The three visions are:

I. The Roll of Destiny, chs. 4 to 11. John finds himself caught up into the presence of God, and sees him seated on his throne, holding out a scroll full of writing but tightly sealed from end to end. No one dares to approach and take the scroll from God's hands, but at length a lamb that has been slain appears and, taking the scroll, begins to break its seals. Dreadful portents attend the breaking of the seals, the angels of invasion, war, famine, and death appear, the martyrs cry to God to deliver them and there is a great earthquake. At the seventh seal, seven angels with trumpets appear, and as each one blows his blast, some fresh calamity develops. When the seventh trumpet is blown, "Loud voices were heard in heaven, saying, 'The sovereignty of the world has passed into the possession of our Lord and of his Christ, and he will reign forever and ever.'"

So the first great act in the drama ends with Christ triumphant.

II. The Dragon War, 12:1 to 19:10. In this second act, in the war between Michael and Satan, Satan has been cast down to the earth, where the conflict is renewed. The prophet looking seaward sees an animal symbolizing the empire come up out of the sea. Then as he looks toward the land he sees another animal coming down from the interior, symbolizing the priesthood of the emperor cult. Between them, they seek to compel people to worship the emperor. A bewildering series of scenes follows; the number of the animal 666 means that the letters of his name (every letter was also a number) add up to that figure, and Nero Cæsar would do that. Domitian was nicknamed Nero for his cruelty, as Juvenal and Martial show. An angel announces the fall of Rome (called Babylon in apocalyptic vocabulary, as in II Esdras). Rome appears as an adulterous woman, seated on seven hills, which are also seven kings—the emperors from Augustus to

Titus; the eighth who is one of the seven is clearly Domitian, conceived as Nero come to life again. Around the burning city, kings, mariners, and merchants lament her overthrow. The vision ends with the renewed prediction of the triumph of the Kingdom of God:

"Then I heard what sounded like the shout of a great multitude and the noise of many waters and the sound of mighty thunders, saying, 'Praise the Lord; for the Lord our God, the Almighty, now reigns.'" The emperor's title in Greek was *Autokrator;* the Greek word for Almighty was *Pantokrator.* The prophet sees that above the Roman Autocrat is the Omnipotent. So the vision ends with a shout of triumph over the final victory.

III. The New Jerusalem, 19:11 to 22:5. Mounted on a white horse, the leader of the heavenly armies, the Word of God, rides forth to victory over the empire. Satan is cast into the abyss, and the martyrs reign with Christ a thousand years. In a final battle God's people triumph, and the great spectacle of the judgment ensues. After it came the new heaven and the new earth, with the New Jerusalem. God's dwelling would be with men, and he would wipe all tears from their eyes. They would live in the city of unspeakable splendor, with its street of gold, its foundations of precious stones, and its gates of pearls. A river flowed through the city, and on its banks grew the tree of life. In the city God's people would worship him, and they would see his face.

Such was the indomitable faith with which the prophet of Patmos sought to inspire his flock in the hour of their greatest peril. Revelation is a book of unconquerable faith in the eventual triumph of the Kingdom of God. John sought to lead the Christians of Asia to take the long look and see what the distant future had in store for the church and the believer. The closing lines, 22:6–21, urge the book upon the churches and reinforce its message.

Read first the letters to the seven churches, chs. 1 to 3, for their pictures of the virtues and the failings of the churches, and the prophet's demands upon them in their perilous times. Then read the visions, the Roll of Destiny, chs. 5 to 11; the Dragon War, 12:1 to 19:10; and the New Jerusalem, 19:11 to 22:5.

Unlike the predictions of the older apocalyptic, John's prophecy is not to be sealed up and stored away for a future generation, but is to be soon fulfilled, 22:10. The conclusion invites mankind to share the sufferings and hopes it describes and demands the preservation of the book unaltered.

In all this you will see the prophet's unshaken confidence that however disasters may crowd upon them one after another, the eventual triumph of their cause is certain. Even the Roman Empire, against which no kingdom or combination of kingdoms had been able to prevail, would go down in ashes before it. This is the magnificent faith of the Revelation, and it is for this that all this stupendous phantasmagoria of apocalyptic imagery is marshaled, to fire the imagination and the faith of the Christians of Asia in their grim battle with persecution.

All through the Christian centuries, and even today, indeed, the Revelation has brought cheer to persecuted groups all over the world, and it still has for the Christian Church a message of unshakable faith in the final triumph of the Kingdom of God.

CHAPTER TWENTY

The Literature of Devotion

O F ALL the books in the world, the Bible is without doubt the most profoundly religious. With all its literary and historical values to which we have called attention, its chief significance for all of us is its amazing sense of the nearness and indeed the presence of God in human life and the reality and importance of that "conversation with the universe" which is for everybody the major part of existence. It is for this that people of every station in every age go to the Bible. It somehow brings them near to God; they even seem to find him in its pages. We turn to the Bible for guidance in moral perplexity, for reinforcement in courageous living, and for comfort in disappointment and loss.

The Bible is rich in passages which lift the reader out of himself into a higher realm filled with the sense of the presence of God, of his care and love, and of the beauty life may take on when it is adjusted to his will. These are the passages that are treasured by every generation of seekers after God. In hours of reflection, by reading or remembering them, we bathe our spirits in their light.

The part of the Old Testament that most signally possesses this quality is the book of Psalms. It has been well said that personal religion finds classical expression in the Psalter. It was the work of many writers; probably more than a hundred are represented in the book, and this gives it the extraordinary range and variety of religious experience it displays. The Psalter has a response to almost any religious mood; it is a veritable treasury of religious experience.

So beyond any other book of the Old Testament, The Psalms has served the religious needs of the Christian Church. It is not the Law, not the histories, not the prophets, but the psalms that have most enriched our devotional life. Generations of Christians have learned them by heart and found comfort and guidance in their familiar words. Other great classics of devotion, such as St. Augustine's *Confessions*, or Thomas à Kempis, or *Pilgrim's Progress*, may no longer help us, but somehow the psalms do not grow old.

The Twenty-third stands foremost: "The Lord is my shepherd." Everyone knows it; it is as familiar as the Lord's Prayer—the one part of the Old Testament of which that can be said. It breathes an atmosphere of trust and comfort. It is supreme among the Psalter's classics of devotion.

What can we put beside it? Certainly the Ninetieth Psalm, "Lord, thou has been our dwelling place in all generations." What are your favorite psalms? It may be well to take stock of the ones that have already made a place for themselves in your religious life. There is also the Forty-sixth: "God is our refuge and strength"; the One Hundred and Third, "Bless the Lord, O my soul"; the Twenty-seventh, "The Lord is my light and my salvation; whom shall I fear?" the Nineteenth, "The heavens are telling the glory of God"; the One Hundred and Twenty-first: "I will lift up mine eyes unto the hills"; and the One Hundred and Thirtieth, "Out of

the depths have I cried unto thee, O Lord!" You will easily
add as many more that you have found companionable, which,
like these, have filled the midnight musings of multitudes of
religious hearts. The Psalms are a great handbook of Christian devotion. And how moving it is to us to think that we can
actually read the very psalms that Jesus and his disciples sang
together before and after the Last Supper, the Hallel, Psalms
113 to 118; 113 and 114 before the Supper:

> "From the rising of the sun unto its setting,
> Let the Lord's name be praised."

And after the Supper, Psalms 115 to 118:

> "Not unto us, O Lord, not unto us,
> But to thy name, give honor. . . .
> Give thanks to the Lord, for he is good,
> For his kindness is everlasting." (Ps. 115:1; 118:29.)

So ended the last hymn Jesus sang.

The Book of Isaiah is also rich in this devotional quality;
poems such as ch. 35:

> "The wilderness and the solitary place shall be glad,
> And the desert shall rejoice, and blossom."

Or such as 40:1–11:

> "Comfort ye, comfort ye my people,
>   saith your God.
> Speak ye comfortably to Jerusalem,
>   and cry unto her,
> That her warfare is accomplished,
>   that her iniquity is pardoned."

Or 42:1–9:

> "Behold my servant, whom I uphold,
> Mine elect, in whom my soul delighteth."

Or chs. 53, or 55, or 60:

> "Arise, shine; for thy light is come,
> And the glory of the Lord is risen upon thee."

Chapter 61 has this quality:

> "The spirit of the Lord God is upon me;
> Because the Lord hath anointed me
> To preach good tidings unto the meek."

—the passage Jesus announced as his text when he preached in Nazareth; or 63:1–6, beginning

> "Who is this that cometh from Edom,
> With dyed garments from Bozrah?"

Nothing could so well illustrate the religious value of the psalms as Jesus' fondness for them and use of them, yet he went far beyond them in his own prayer and his Beatitudes. For above them all stands the Lord's Prayer, so close to us and so much a part of us that it is hard to think of it objectively, as brought to us by the Bible, in the Gospel of Matthew. Its seven brief petitions declare our reverence, dedication, submission, and repentance, and our need of food, forgiveness, and moral strength. When we utter it, we are at once lifted out of the selfishness and pettiness that so often creep into our prayers, into the regions where Jesus himself lived and worked. It is only fifty-four words long, but nowhere else is so much done in so few words for the religious life of mankind.

The Beatitudes are themselves a psalm, and might be called the Psalm of Jesus. They are cast in the style of so many psalms that begin like them with "Blessed." But the Beatitudes ring out with new standards of blessedness, for they bless the poor, the bereaved, the humble, the hungry, and the persecuted, Matt. 5:3–12. So they have taken a place with the Lord's Prayer in Christian devotion. That Jesus should have expressed himself in this way, so characteristic of the psalms of the Old Testament, shows his devotion to the Psalter.

Many sayings of Jesus have this uplifting, comforting power. "Come unto me, all ye that labour and are heavy laden, and I will give you rest. Take my yoke upon you, and learn of me; for I am meek and lowly in heart: and ye shall find rest unto your souls. For my yoke is easy, and my burden is light." (Matt. 11:28–30.)

The Gospel of John is especially rich in such expression. Everyone knows that great sentence in 3:16, "For God so loved the world, that he gave his only begotten son, that whosoever believeth in him should not perish, but have everlasting life." And among the very greatest classics of devotion are the Upper Room discourses in John, chs. 14 to 16:

"Let not your heart be troubled; believe in God, believe also in me. There are many rooms in my Father's house. . . . I have loved you just as the Father has loved me. You must retain my love. . . . The command that I give you is to love one another just as I have loved you. No one can show greater love than by giving up his life for his friends. You are my friends if you do what I command you. . . . What I command you to do is to love one another." (John 14:1; 15:9, 12–14.)

This is exactly the atmosphere of the First Letter of John:

"Dear friends, let us love one another, for love comes from God, and everyone who loves is a child of God and knows God. Whoever does not love does not know God, for God is love. . . . Dear friends, if God has loved us so, we ought to love one another. . . . We love because he first loved us. . . . This is the command that we get from him, that whoever loves God must love his brother also." (I John 4:7, 8, 11, 19, 21.)

Nothing is more characteristic of the Bible than its wealth in just this kind of literature. It is, in fact, one of the supreme values of the Bible, although by no means the only one.

Everyone must make his own selection of the passages in the Bible that impress him as possessing this mysterious quality. There are those great benedictions, which have spoken and still speak peace to so many hearts, such as the old Hebrew one which the priests were to use in blessing the people, Num. 6:24–26:

> "The Lord bless you, and keep you!
> The Lord make his face shine upon you, and be gracious unto you!
> The Lord lift up his countenance upon you, and give you peace!"

Or the words of Paul to the Philippians, 4:7:

"The peace of God, which passes all understanding, shall keep your hearts and minds through Jesus Christ."

How triumphantly Paul puts this in concluding his great argument in Romans!

"Then what shall we conclude from this? If God is for us, who can be against us? Will not he who did not spare his own Son, but gave him up for us all, with that gift give us everything? . . . Who can separate us from Christ's love? Can trouble or misfortune or persecution or hunger or destitution or danger or the sword? . . . But in all these things we are more than victorious through him who loved us." (Rom. 8:31, 32, 35, 37.)

Then there is the thirteenth chapter of I Corinthians:

"If I can speak the languages of men and even of angels, but have no love, I am only a noisy gong or a clashing cymbal."

Parts of the great fifteenth chapter also possess this quality with their strong faith in a future life:

"For this perishable nature must put on the imperishable, and this mortal nature must put on immortality." (I Cor. 15:53.)

John in the Revelation heard a loud voice say:

"God's dwelling is with men, and he will live with them. They will be his people and God himself will be with them, and he will wipe every tear from their eyes. There will be no death any longer, nor any grief or crying or pain. The old order has passed away." (Rev. 21:3, 4.)

And what splendid confidence and indomitable faith, in the face of persecution and disaster, find expression in the chorus that concludes the second vision in the Revelation, 19:6:

"Then I heard what sounded like the shout of a great multitude and the noise of many waters and the sound of mighty thunders, saying,

"Hallelujah, for the Lord God, the Almighty, now reigns!"

CHAPTER TWENTY-ONE

The Historical Background

ALTHOUGH we have tried to set the books of the Bible in their historical situations, as necessary to the full understanding of them, a coherent sketch of their background in history will help the reader to see them in their successive settings.

The Hebrews, enslaved and overworked in Egypt by Rameses II, in the thirteenth century before Christ, escaped from the country toward 1200 B.C. in Merneptah's reign and, after a generation of nomadic life in the desert, entered Palestine. It was probably then that they adopted its language, Hebrew, which used an alphabet adapted from that of the Phœnicians on the seacoast. In the course of the conquest of the Land of Canaan, Deborah uttered her song, later committed to writing, and preserved in the fifth chapter of Judges. It was probably composed about 1150 B.C. and is the oldest poem of such length in the Bible.

While the dates for this earliest period are not certain, the kingdom was probably organized under Saul in 1028 B.C., and David's reign covered the forty years from 1013 to 973. He took Jerusalem and made it the capital of the twelve tribes. Solomon, too, reigned forty years, about 973–933, in greater splendor, and built the Temple in Jerusalem. But at his death the northern ten tribes, led by Jeroboam, who had been Solomon's manager of labor, revolted to form a new Kingdom of Israel, leaving only Benjamin and Judah in the Southern Kingdom, the Kingdom of Judah, with the old capital, Jerusalem. The Northern Kingdom was known as Israel, and the Southern as Judah. Written accounts later used in Judges and Samuel were taking shape as early as the tenth century B.C.

The Dynasty of Jeroboam, 933–911. Under its king Jeroboam, 933–912, the Northern Kingdom, with its capital at Shechem, began a career that soon overshadowed Judah's, though its history was marked by an unending series of usurpations and assassinations. Jeroboam's son Nadab, 912–911, was murdered after a reign of only two years.

The Dynasty of Baasha, 911–887. A usurper named Baasha now took the throne and moved his capital to Tirzah. He reigned from 911 to 888, but his son and successor Elah had reigned hardly two years when he was killed by one of his officers named Zimri, who made himself king.

The Dynasty of Omri, 887–843. After one bloody week of rule Zimri was swept aside by Omri, the general of the army, who took the throne, 887–875. He strengthened and extended the kingdom and built Samaria for his capital. His son Ahab, 875–853, who married the Tyrian princess Jezebel, found an antagonist in the Prophet Elijah, and fell in battle with the king of Syria. Ahaziah, 853–852 and Joram, 852–843, concluded the dynasty of Omri. In their time Mesha, king of Moab, successfully rebelled against Israel and in celebration of his success erected the Moabite Stone, our oldest considerable Hebrew inscription, probably about 840.

The Dynasty of Jehu, 843–744. Jehu, Ahab's general, was urged to usurp the throne by Elijah's famous successor Elisha. Jehu, 843–816, paid tribute to Assyria as recorded on the famous black obelisk of Shalmaneser III, erected not long after 842, and lost Israel's territory east of the Jordan to the king of Damascus, but he wiped out the house of Ahab and the worshipers of Baal from Samaria. After two reigns of little consequence, Jehoahaz, 816–800, and Jehoash, 800–785, Jeroboam II began his long and prosperous reign, 785–744, materially the golden age of the Northern Kingdom. He won back from Damascus the country east of the Jordan, since Assyria was pressing Damascus on the east. Traditions of Israel's past were taking written shape in Israel in his time, but the social and economic evils of his day stirred Amos to prophesy, 765–750.

Anarchy and Confusion, 744–721. But a new usurper named Shallum made short work of Jeroboam's son Zechariah, only to give way at once to a series of adventurers in royalty—Menahem, 744–738 (the times of Hosea), Pekahiah, 738–737, Pekah, 737–733, and Hoshea, 733–722. But even in stronger hands Israel would have been powerless before the rising might of Assyria under Tiglath-pileser III, 745–727; and his successors Shalmaneser V, 727–722, and Sargon, 722–705, completed the destruction of the Northern Kingdom, taking Samaria in 722 and in 721 carrying more than twenty-seven thousand of its people off to exile in Mesopotamia. From this disaster the Northern Kingdom never recovered, nor did the ten tribes ever return to revive their national life.

Meantime, the southern part of Solomon's kingdom, which had been reduced to the Kingdom of Judah, went on its way under a long succession of descendants of David, so that at its end it was possible to trace an unbroken line of Davidic kings from David's accession in 1013 B.C. to Jehoiachin in 597 B.C. and his brother and successor Zedekiah, 597–586, a period of four hundred and twenty-seven years. Few dynasties, ancient or modern, have endured so long.

The Dynasty of David, 1013 to 586 B.C. After the reigns of David, 1013–973 B.C., and Solomon, 973–933, Solomon's son Rehoboam became king.

The Kingdom of Judah, from the rebellion of Israel to Israel's capture of Jerusalem, 933–780. The high-handed severity of Rehoboam, 933–917, gave Jeroboam his opportunity to detach the ten tribes of the north and form the Kingdom of Israel. But Rehoboam maintained himself in David's city of Jerusalem. Judah went on with varying fortunes under Abijah, 917–915, Asa, 915–875, and Jehoshaphat, 875–851.

Already old records and traditions were taking shape in Judah in a narrative that later was brought into the early parts of the Pentateuch. Jehoshaphat's son Jehoram, 851–844, married Athaliah, the daughter of Ahab and Jezebel, and upon the death of Ahaziah in 843, Athaliah took control and almost succeeded in blotting out the Davidic line, but Jehoash was saved and became king, 837–798. His successor Amaziah, 798–780, made war upon Israel but was badly beaten, and Jerusalem was captured and half destroyed.

A new era, 780–586 B.C., began with Azariah, or Uzziah, 780–740, who refortified Jerusalem and restored Judah's prosperity. The year of his death witnessed Isaiah's appearance as a prophet, 740–701. His work continued under Jotham, 740–735, Ahaz, 735–720, who became a vassal of Assyria, and Hezekiah, 720–692, who chose to side with her enemies. In contrast with Hezekiah, Manasseh, 692–639, suppressed the prophets and favored idolatry. His successor Amon, 639–638, was soon assassinated, and with Josiah, 638–607, the worship of Jehovah was resumed. A new era in Hebrew religion began with the finding of Deuteronomy in the Temple in 621 B.C. and its adoption as the religious law book. Those days witnessed the prophecies of Zephaniah, 627 B.C. and the beginning of Jeremiah's prophetic work in the same year. Assyria was now hastening to her end; in 612 Nineveh fell before the Babylonians, as described by Nahum.

Josiah met his death at Megiddo in 607, resisting invasion by Necho II, Pharaoh of Egypt, who removed his successor Jehoahaz after a reign of three months and recognized Jehoiakim as king, 607–597 B.C. But the Babylonians were now rising to power and they took Judah over from the Egyptians in 604, and when Jehoiakim tried to break away from their control in 598, they besieged Jerusalem and took it, in 597 B.C. Jehoiakim had died during the siege and it was his son Jehoiachin (597) who surrendered the city, and was taken off to a long captivity, 597–561 B.C., in Babylon. Zedekiah, another son of Josiah, was placed on the throne in 597, but he became involved in dealings with Egypt, and the Babylonians returned in 586 B.C. to destroy Jerusalem and put an end to Judah's national existence. This is the tragic story reflected in so much of The Book of Jeremiah.

The period of the Exile, 597–538 B.C., finds expression in parts of Jeremiah, in Ezekiel, and in parts of Isaiah, especially chs. 40 to 55. It was terminated by the rise of the Persians under Cyrus, who took Babylon in 538 B.C. and gave the Hebrews permission to return to Palestine. Some responded and went. A few years later another party returned and, led by Haggai and Zechariah, 520–519, the Hebrews rebuilt the Temple, 516 B.C. Under Nehemiah, 444, the city walls were restored, and in 397 Ezra the Scribe brought the completed Law from Babylon and read it to the people, whose leaders solemnly adopted it.

Alexander's defeat of Darius at Issus, and the resultant conquest of Palestine, 333 B.C., ended the Persian domination and brought the Jews under Greek control. At Alexander's death, 323, it became part of the Egyptian empire of the Ptolemies, but in 198 B.C. it was transferred to the Syrian kingdom of the Seleucidæ. The efforts of King Antiochus Epiphanes, 175–164 B.C., to impose Greek manners and culture upon the Jews led to the Maccabæan uprising of 168, which under the leadership of Judas Maccabæus restored their religious freedom, 165. Political independence came later, in 141, as a result of the leadership of Judas' brothers Jonathan, 160–143, and Simon, 143–135, after four hundred and fifty years of subjection. It was under Simon's son John Hyrcanus, 135–103 B.C., that the Pharisees came into prominence as a party. Alexander Jannæus was the next ruler of importance, 103–76. He was a vigorous opponent of the Pharisees, and it was probably in his reign that I Maccabees, the Sadducean story of the nation's liberation, was written. Alexander's widow, Alexandra, who succeeded him, 76–67, took the opposite course and favored the Pharisees; probably in her day the Pharisaic history II Maccabees appeared.

But the feuds that rose among the Hasmonæan princes, as the Maccabees were called, opened the way for the Idumæans and the Romans to intervene in Palestinian affairs, and in 63 B.C. Pompey entered Jerusalem as its master. An

Idumæan, Herod the Great, the husband of the Hasmonæan princess Mariamne, ruled the country as king under the Romans, 39–4 B.C. It was near the end of his reign that Jesus was born, 4 or 6 B.C. After Herod's death, his son Archelaus ruled Judea, Samaria, and Idumæa (Edom) for ten years, 4 B.C.–A.D. 6, though without the title of king. His brother Herod Antipas was made governor of Galilee and Perea, and held that office for forty years, 4 B.C.–A.D. 37. He is often mentioned in the Gospels and The Acts; he had John the Baptist put to death and shared in the conviction of Jesus, Luke 23:7–15.

In A.D. 39 his territory was assigned to Herod Agrippa I, a grandson of Herod and Mariamne, and so a descendant of the Maccabees. He was given the title of king, and in A.D. 41 was given Judea, too, so that his kingdom virtually reached the proportions of that of his grandfather, Herod the Great. He is mentioned in Acts, ch. 12. He died in A.D. 44.

His son Herod Agrippa II was made king of Chalcis in A.D. 49, and was shifted in 53 to a larger realm including Galilee and Perea, which he ruled until about 100. It was before him that Paul made his famous defense, in Acts, ch. 26.

In the time of Jesus' ministry Galilee was governed by Roman procurators, as it had been from A.D. 6 on. They were Coponius, probably A.D. 6–9; Marcus Ambivius, probably 9–12; Annius Rufus, probably 12–15; Valerius Gratus, 15–26; Pontius Pilate, who condemned Jesus to death, 26–36; Marcellus, 36–37; and Marullus, 37–41.

Then, after the reign of Herod Agrippa I, A.D. 41 to 44, came a second series of procurators, Cuspius Fadus, 44–?; Tiberius Alexander, ?–48; Ventidius Cumanus, 48–52; Antonius Felix (before whom Paul appeared, Acts, ch. 24), a freedman, brother of Nero's favorite Pallas, 52–58; Porcius Festus (who brought Paul before Agrippa, Acts, ch. 26), 58–62; Albinus, 62–64; and Florus, 64–66, under whom the Jewish revolt broke out, 66–70.

Another Roman governor mentioned in the narrative of Acts (18:12) was Gallio, the brother of Seneca and uncle of the Roman poet Lucan. He was proconsul of Greece (Achaia) in A.D. 51–52, which enables us to fix the date of I Thessalonians, the earliest piece of Christian literature that we possess, in the spring of 50.

Back of these minor figures were the great rulers of the Roman world, the emperors; Augustus, 31 B.C.–A.D. 14, in whose reign Jesus was born; Tiberius, 14–37, in whose reign Jesus was crucified; Gaius, 37–41; Claudius, 41–54, mentioned in Acts 11:28, in whose reign Paul began to write his letters; Nero, 54–68, to whose court Paul was sent for trial; Galba, 68–69; Otho, 69; Vitellius, 69; Vespasian, 69–79, the time of the writing of the Gospel of Mark; Titus, 79–81, the probable time of the writing of the Gospel of Matthew; Domitian, 81–96, the time of the writing of the Gospel of Luke, The Acts, the Revelation, Hebrews, and I Peter; Nerva, 96–98; Trajan, 98–117, the time of the writing of the Gospel and letters of John; Hadrian, 117–138; Antoninus Pius, 138–161, when the Pastoral Letters and II Peter were written.

TABLES OF REIGNS AND PERIODS IN OFFICE

KINGS

Of All Israel:

	B.C.
Saul	1028–1013.
David	1013–973.
Solomon	973–933.

Of Israel, the Northern Kingdom:

	B.C.
Jeroboam	933–912.
Nadab	912–911.
Baasha	911–888.
Elah	888–887.
Zimri	887.
Omri	887–875.
Ahab	875–853.
Ahaziah	853–852.
Joram	852–843.
Jehu	843–816.
Jehoahaz	816–800.
Jehoash	800–785.
Jeroboam II	785–744.
Zechariah	744.
Shallum	744.
Menahem	744–738.
Pekahiah	738–737.
Pekah	737–733.
Hoshea	733–722.

Israel conquered by Assyria and carried into exile, 722–721 B.C.

Of Judah, the Southern Kingdom:

	B.C.
Rehoboam	933–917.
Abijah	917–915.
Asa	915–875.
Jehoshaphat	875–851.
Jehoram	851–844.
Ahaziah	844–843.
Athaliah	843–837.
Jehoash	837–798.
Amaziah	798–780.
Uzziah (Azariah)	780–740.
Jotham	740–735.
Ahaz	735–720.
Hezekiah	720–692.
Manasseh	692–639.
Amon	639–638.
Josiah	638–607.
Jehoahaz	607.
Jehoiakim	607–597.
Jehoiachin	597.
Zedekiah	597–586.

Jerusalem destroyed by the Babylonians, 586 B.C.

The Exile, 597–538 B.C.

After the Babylonian (597–538 B.C.), Persian (538–333 B.C.), and Greek (Macedonian, Egyptian, Syrian, 333–168 B.C.) domination:

The Maccabæans or Hasmonæans:

B.C.

Judas Maccabæus
                    168–160.
Jonathan   160–143.
Simon   143–135.
John Hyrcanus 135–103.
Alexander Jannæus
                    103–76.
Alexandra   76–67.
(Intervention of Pompey,
        63.)
Herod the Great,
    king   39–4.
Archelaus, ethnarch
        4 B.C.–A.D. 6.

Roman Procurators of Judea:

A.D.

Coponius   6–9.
                    (probably)
Marcus Ambivius 9–12.
                    (probably)
Annius Rufus   12–15.
                    (probably)
Valerius Gratus 15–26.
Pontius Pilate   26–36.
Marcellus   36–37.
Marullus   37–41.
(Herod Agrippa I,
        king 41-44.)

Roman Procurators of Judea:

Cuspius Fadus   44–?.
Tiberius Alexander
            ?–48.
Ventidius Cumanus
            48–52.
Antonius Felix   52–58.
Porcius Festus   58–62.
Albinus   62–64.
Florus   64–66.

Roman Emperors:

Augustus 31 B.C.–A.D. 14.
              A.D.
Tiberius   14–37.
Gaius   37–41.
Claudius   41–54.
Nero   54–68.
Galba   68–69.
Otho   69.
Vitellius   69.
Vespasian   69–79.
Titus   79–81.
Domitian   81–96.
Nerva   96–98.
Trajan   98–117.
Hadrian   117–138.
Antoninus Pius 138–161.

CHAPTER TWENTY·TWO

Chronological Reading

W E HAVE thus far approached the reading of the Bible from its angle of greatest interest—the biographical angle, beginning with its greatest personalities, first of all Jesus. But there is another way of reading it which has values of its own, and that is the chronological reading of the books in the order in which they were probably written, so that their great ideas and their religious discoveries emerge before the reader in the order in which they first burst upon mankind. It is true, we cannot always date the composition of these books definitely, but most of the prophets clearly reflect the times in which they wrote, and in general we can be fairly sure when the other books were completed. This list will show when the prophets did their work and when the other books reached completion. For another reading of the Bible, therefore, take its books up chronologically, in the following order:

The Old Testament

B.C.

765–750 Amos
745–735 Hosea

224

B.C.

	730–721	Micah
	740–701	Isaiah
Ca.	650	Deuteronomy
	627	Zephaniah
	627–586	Jeremiah
	612	Nahum
	608–597	Habakkuk
	592–567	Ezekiel
Ca.	550	I, II Samuel, I, II Kings
	520, 519	Haggai
	520, 519	Zechariah
Ca.	475–450	Malachi
	444–432	Nehemiah
Ca.	450–400	Obadiah
Ca.	400	Judges
Ca.	400	Job
Ca.	400	Joel
Ca.	400	The Pentateuch, Genesis to Deuteronomy
Ca.	375–350	Ruth
Ca.	375–350	Joshua
Ca.	350	Jonah
Ca.	325–300	I, II Chronicles, Nehemiah, Ezra
Ca.	300–200	Proverbs
Ca.	300–200	Lamentations
Ca.	200–150	Ecclesiastes

The Apocrypha

Ca. 300–200	Soon after 200	Tobit
	Ca. 175	Ecclesiasticus
Ca. 165	Daniel	168	Prayer of Azariah
Ca. 150	Psalms	Ca. 150	Song of Three Children

B.C.   *The Apocrypha*

Ca. 150	Esther	Ca. 150	I Esdras
		Ca. 150	Judith
		Ca. 150–100	Prayer of Manasseh
		100	Additions to Esther
		Ca. 100–75	Susanna
		Ca. 100–75	Bel and the Dragon
		Ca. 100–75	I Maccabees
		Ca. 75–65	II Maccabees
		A.D.	
		38–41	Wisdom of Solomon

The New Testament

A.D.

	50, 51	I, II Thessalonians
	53	Galatians
	54, 55	I, II Corinthians
	56, 57	Romans
	59, 60	Philippians
	60, 61	Colossians, Philemon
		Ca. 66–270 II Esdras
Ca.	70	Gospel of Mark
Ca.	80	Gospel of Matthew
Ca.	90	Gospel of Luke, Acts of the Apostles
	90–93	Ephesians
Ca.	95	Revelation

A.D.		*The Apocrypha*	
Ca. 95	Hebrews		
Ca. 95	I Peter		
Ca. 100	James	Ca. 100	Baruch
		Ca. 100	Letter of Jeremiah
Ca. 110	I, II, III John		
Ca. 110	Gospel of John		
Ca. 125	Jude		
Ca. 150	I, II Timothy, Titus		
Ca. 160	II Peter		

CHAPTER TWENTY-THREE

English Bibles

1382   John Wyclif, the first English Bible.

1525   William Tyndale, the first New Testament printed in English.

1535   Miles Coverdale, the first Bible printed in English.

1537   John Rogers, the first Licensed English Bible.

1539   Richard Taverner, "The Most Sacred Bible."

1539   The Great Bible (the Chained Bible), the first Authorized English Bible.

1560   The Geneva or Breeches Bible, the Puritan Bible.

1568   The Bishops' Bible, the second Authorized English Bible.

1582   The Rheims New Testament, beginning the Catholic Bible.

1610   The Douai Old Testament, completing the Catholic Bible.

1611   The King James Bible, the third Authorized English Bible.

1615–1769   King James Bible repeatedly tacitly revised, T. Paris, 1762; B. Blayney, 1769.

1729–1905   Numerous Private Translations, principally of the New Testament.

1749 Richard Challoner's revision of the Catholic Douay Bible.

1885 The English Revised Version, the fourth Authorized English Bible.

1898–1945 The Modern Speech translations.

1901 The American Standard Version.

1941 The Catholic Revised New Testament, an Authorized version.

1946 The Revised Standard Version of the New Testament.

Anyone who proposes to read the Bible is, of course, faced with the question, What Bible? For the Bible was written in Hebrew and Greek, and without an extensive knowledge of these languages no one can read it except in somebody's translation of it. And for fifteen hundred years it has been read principally in translations.

First in Latin translations, which were revised by Jerome about A.D. 382–400 into the Latin Vulgate, the authorized Bible of Europe and Britain for more than a thousand years, and still the Bible of the Catholic Church. In A.D. 1382 John Wyclif translated it into English, and his work was revised soon after by John Purvey, and circulated in manuscripts, for that was before the time of printed books.

But the real beginning of the Bible in English as we know it was made by William Tyndale, who was stirred by the example of Luther, the trumpet call of Erasmus for translations of the Bible into all the living languages, and above all by the religious needs of the English people, and in 1525 printed a translation of the New Testament made directly from the Greek into the spoken English of his day.

More than any other man, William Tyndale created the religious vocabulary of English Protestantism, and nine-tenths of his New Testament still lives in the New Testament of the King James Version. His spelling, however, had all the freedom of his times, for he could spell the word "it" in twelve different ways, all of them correct.

Tyndale went on to learn Hebrew and began to translate the Old Testament, publishing his version of the first five books of it, Genesis to Deuteronomy in 1530, and of Jonah in 1531.

In 1535, while Tyndale was in prison in Belgium, Miles Coverdale put forth the first complete English Bible to appear in print. He put into it Tyndale's New Testament and his Old Testament as far as he had printed it, that is, the Pentateuch and Jonah. The rest Coverdale frankly translated from the best Latin and German versions he could find. But the Coverdale Bible was the first Bible printed in English.

Tyndale was put to death for his Reformation views in 1536, but in 1537 his last friend, John Rogers, published the second English Bible, using Tyndale's translation of the New Testament and of the first half of the Old, Genesis to II Chronicles. For the rest of the Bible, Rogers simply revised Coverdale. This was the first licensed English Bible; it could lawfully be bought and sold, and owned and read.

In 1539 two more English Bibles appeared, one, Richard Taverner's revision of John Rogers' Bible, the other Miles Coverdale's revision of it, made by order of the English bishops for use in public worship. This Great Bible, as it was called from its size, was made to be read in church, and so was the first English Authorized Bible. It took its place at once upon the lecterns of English churches, instead of the Latin Vulgate version, which had been read in church so long.

These four Bibles printed in four years show the zeal of Reformation England for the Bible in a tongue the people could understand.

In 1560 the Puritans who had fled to Geneva produced a thorough revision of the Bible, the Geneva or Breeches Bible, so called from its reading that Adam and Eve "sewed figtre leaves together, and made themselves breeches," in Gen. 3:7. It was broken into the new numbered paragraphs or verses devised by Robert Estienne in 1551, and was the first Bible to appear not in the old black letter but in the graceful new Roman type, in universal use today. It became the household Bible of England, and between 1560 and 1644 passed through more than a hundred and forty editions. It was the Bible of Shakespeare and of the Puritans.

It stirred Archbishop Matthew Parker to undertake a revision of the Great Bible into the Bishops' Bible of 1568, the second authorized English Bible, which now replaced the Great Bible in use in public worship.

Ten years later Gregory Martin, a member of the Catholic college in Rheims, began his translation of the Latin Vulgate into English, and in 1582 his New Testament was published. His Old Testament did not appear until 1610, when the college had removed to Douai. It completed the Catholic English Bible, which is generally known as the Douay Bible.

Meantime in 1604 plans had been made with King James's approval for a revision of the Bishops' Bible, and in 1611 the new version appeared, the product of the labors of the best Greek and Hebrew scholars in the English universities. Its stately English reflected the amazing progress English as a literary language had made in the sixteenth century, and still delights the cultivated ear. It was the third Authorized English Bible, replacing the Bishops' Bible in church use and soon surpassing the Geneva in popular favor.

To many it seems that this completes the story of the English Bible, but it is not so. For hardly had the King James Bible made its appearance when, in 1628, a fifth-century manuscript of the Greek Bible reached London from Constantinople, a gift from the Patriarch Cyril Lucar to the King. English scholars perceived that its text of the New Testament was from five to ten centuries earlier than that of the manuscripts Erasmus had used in his Greek Testament, on which all English translations up to that time had been principally based.

In the century that followed, other Greek manuscripts of similar antiquity came to light and led to the appearance in the eighteenth century of a long series of translations by individual scholars, such as William Whiston, the translator of Josephus, 1745, John Wesley, 1755, and many others. These private versions, as they may be called, are usually passed over in complete silence by historians of the English Bible and form a forgotten chapter in its history. But they had an important influence upon its development; the more so as more and more ancient manuscripts continued, as they still continue, to be found.

In the early years of the nineteenth century the Vatican manuscript of the Greek Bible came to the attention of Greek Biblical scholars, who awoke to its extraordinary value and importance, and in 1859 Tischendorf's discovery of the Sinaitic codex in St. Catharine's convent on Mount Sinai brought the whole matter to a head. For in the light of these discoveries the Convocation of Canterbury, the southern part of the Church of England, in 1870 voted to revise the King James Version, and in 1881 the English Revised New Testament made its appearance. It was followed in 1885 by the Revised Old Testament, and a revision of the Apocrypha appeared in 1894.

The Apocrypha formed an integral part of the King James Version of 1611, and are still occasionally found in Oxford and Cambridge Bibles, even in those of convenient size for personal reading. They are also published separately. The Revised Version of them (1894) is available in a convenient little volume published in a series of the World's Classics.

The English Revised Version was the fourth Authorized English Bible. It was meant to be a very conservative revision of the King James Version, its first principle being to change the 1611 text only as far as the meaning of the original required. Its second was that in making such changes expressions at least as old as those of 1611 should be used. The result was that its diction was actually more antique than that of the King James.

An American revision committee to coöperate with the British committee had been organized by Dr. Philip Schaff, of Union Theological Seminary, in New York, and exchanged recommended readings with the committee in England throughout its work. Many of its recommendations were accepted, others were put in the margin. The American committee was informed that after the lapse of fourteen years it might publish its own revision, and so in 1901 appeared the American Standard Version, embodying the readings of the American Committee.

It was understood that its publisher, Thomas Nelson &

Sons, in New York, should, after holding the copyright for twenty-eight years, turn it over to some undenominational Protestant body. In 1929 Nelson transferred it to the International Council of Religious Education. That body inquired of the seminaries as to men competent to form a revision committee and in accordance with their advice assembled a new revision committee of eight Old Testament and eight New Testament scholars, besides two or three others especially familiar with the needs of public worship. It was known as the American Standard Bible Revision Committee. The full committee had its first meeting in the spring of 1930, but ceased to meet in 1932, as a result of the depression.

Not long after, however, a Catholic group, the Confraternity of Christian Doctrine, was organized in Kansas City and seven years later published a new revision of the Douay version (previously revised by Challoner, in 1749), based upon the Latin Vulgate. This was put forth as an Authorized Version, accepted for use in public worship in Catholic churches in this country. It represented a great advance upon the Douay in every respect. While by no means in modern speech, it moved somewhat in that direction, changing "ye" to "you" and giving up the antique forms of the third person, "goeth," "willeth," and the like. It also showed acquaintance with the best modern-speech translations of the Greek. Since its appearance in May, 1941, a papal encyclical has encouraged Catholic translators to make use of the original languages as well as the Latin Vulgate in further translations, and this will no doubt affect their work on the Old Testament now in progress.

The American Standard Revision Committee was again called together in 1938, and reorganized. Some of the older men had died, others had resigned from the Committee, which thus found itself considerably altered in personnel and attitude. The new group had felt the effect of the wave of modern-speech translations of the New Testament called forth by the discoveries of great numbers of Greek papyrus documents of the first and second centuries, which so much resemble the Greek of the New Testament. Fifty years have passed since that resemblance was first noted, and in that time at least fifty modern-speech translations of the New Testament have appeared. They have had a warm welcome and reached and met the needs of millions of readers. The reorganized Revision Committee felt that their revision must take advantage of this new movement and bring its methods to bear on its task.

The result was that the Revised Standard Version of the New Testament, which came out on February 11, 1946, was in the main a modern-speech version and was warmly welcomed by great numbers of people who had come to feel that such a version brought the New Testament message most forcibly home to their minds.

The modern reader is, therefore, more richly supplied with forms of the New Testament from which to choose than any English reader has ever been. Many still prefer the antique diction of the sixteenth century that forms most of the great King James Version of 1611. Even it has been greatly altered in spelling, proper names, and even vocabulary to some extent in the long line of tacit revisions through which it has passed.

The English Revised Version of 1885 and the American Standard Version of 1901 have retained most of the antiqueness of the King James, which the modern-speech translations have cast off. Still more recently, the Revised Standard New Testament has moved markedly in this direction (1946), as the *Twentieth-Century New Testament* (1901–05), Weymouth (1903), Moffatt (1913), the American translation (1923), and others had done in more thoroughgoing fashion before it. Particularly for the letters of Paul, so obscure in the King James and the revised versions of 1885 and 1901, the modern versions are indispensable. For the Old Testament, neither the Catholic nor the Protestant revisions has yet appeared; the Protestant is promised for 1950. The English Revision of 1885 included the Old Testament, as did the American Standard of 1901. The Jewish Council of American Rabbis in 1917 produced a revision of the English Old Testament, but it could hardly be called a new translation, as it followed the King James and the revisions in the main. The Moffatt translation of 1924–1925 brought great vigor and clarity to the Old Testament, as did the American translation, edited by Dr. J. M. P. Smith, 1927. Both undoubtedly do much to make the difficult prophetic books more readily intelligible to the reader.

The Apocrypha have been almost entirely neglected by revisers; the English Revision of 1894 did very little to improve them, and the American Revision of 1901 left them absolutely untouched. The American translation of 1938, the only one based directly on the Greek throughout (except for II Esdras, which exists only in Latin), is the only fresh version of the whole group of fourteen books made since Coverdale's Bible translated them in 1535. No book owes more, however, to modern manuscript discovery, for Bensly in 1875 published no less than seventy verses of the seventh chapter of II Esdras, found in an Amiens manuscript, but unknown to earlier translators, and so absent from all previous English versions.

Fifty years ago Richard Green Moulton, in his *Modern Reader's Bible*, did much to bring out the fact that the Bible is not a book but a library of sixty-six, or with the Apocrypha, eighty, different books. It was to accomplish this that he published it in twenty-four small volumes. He made use of the English Revised Version of 1885, but his intelligent paragraphing and arrangement made such a difference in the text that most people to this day suppose he made a new translation.

For many years past another form of Bible publication has been assuming considerable proportions. It is the Short Bible, a volume of selections designed to attract readers who have been repelled by the sheer bulk of the whole Bible. These books are not meant as substitutes for the Bible but as approaches to it.

It is sometimes thought that the rise of new versions confuses and perplexes the public, but that is not their main effect. They are intended to bring home to the modern reader more of the clearness and vigor the books of the Bible had for their first publics, in the ancient times when they were written. Certainly in the older English versions whole areas like the Minor Prophets (who were minor only in bulk, not in meaning or value) or the letters of Paul remain largely unintelligible to the general reader. He may still enjoy the sound of them, so familiar to him from his childhood, but he must not make the dangerous mistake of confusing familiarity with comprehension.

Nor are these older versions better for the literary study of the Bible as is sometimes affirmed. The King James Version is undoubtedly a great monument of English literature of the sixteenth and early seventeenth centuries. That is one thing. But it is not curiosity about English literature that leads most of us to the Bible; it is our religious needs.

On the other hand, for devotional purposes many who have been brought up on the King James or the older revisions, English and American, will find their wording coming back to memory freighted with old religious associations, and these are values not to be gainsaid. So the present wealth of Bible translations enriches our varied uses of the Bible, the religious treasure house of mankind.

Index

Index

A

B

C

D